CHEZ MANON

À Fleur et Raphaël, mes petits coeurs

CHEZ MANON

Simple recipes from a French home Kitchen

Manon Lagrève

Hardie Grant
BOOKS

Chez Manon

Hello and welcome to *Chez Manon*! In this book, I'm taking you on a journey to my childhood home in Brittany, to explore my family's cooking, traditions and *joie de vivre*. Then I am bringing you back to London, where I use my French roots and food values to create simple and nutritious recipes for everyday life.

My childhood home is based in the heart of a small village of 3,000 souls in Brittany, made up of a large church, three *boulangeries*, two *bouchers/charcutiers*, one *crêperie*, two *épiceries*, two restaurants and one weekly *marché* on a Friday. I know – it sounds like the classic French villages you may have seen in the movies.

But this is not a movie. People don't see eating good-quality food as a privilege or a luxury, it is simply the only way that they live: eating seasonally, often growing fruit trees or keeping a vegetable patch in their garden, or at least some fresh herbs, and some even having the bonus of a couple of hens for fresh eggs.

La Qualité avant Tout

Quality Before Everything

My parents are farmers, just like my grandparents, just like my great-grandparents, and even further down my family tree. My *mamie* – my grandmother – always said 'when times were hard, people came to the countryside for food.' My upbringing has given me so much respect for farmers, the work they do and the quality food they produce throughout the seasons. (I do realize, of course, that this is not as clear a conclusion in many countries, where agriculture isn't as controlled as it is in Europe, and farming practices are clearly damaging to the planet, damaging to the animals and, in the end, damaging to those who eat the produce.) But I am lucky enough to have been brought up valuing quality above everything.

Another important factor is that we respect the seasonality of ingredients, which means, when we eat them, they taste at their best and are the most affordable. Buying locally is another advantage as you avoid transportation miles and their environmental impact. But in this book, I'm taking you to London where I live now! It is much harder to find local and seasonal ingredients in cities than in my village in Brittany. This is why *Chez Manon* uses ingredients that are widely available in supermarkets or your local grocery store, so you can easily recreate the recipes wherever you are, and bring French-inspired food into your home.

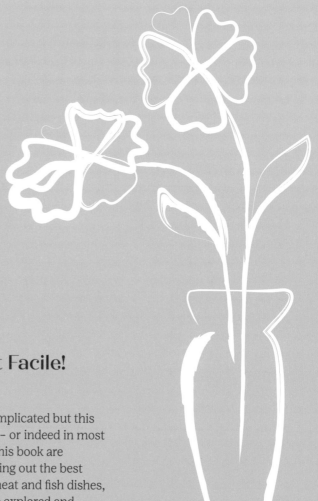

La Cuisine Française c'est Facile!

Demystifying French Home Food

French food is sometimes seen as being complicated but this is certainly not true of cooking *Chez Manon* – or indeed in most French households. Most of the recipes in this book are astonishingly simple and are designed to bring out the best in the ingredients. You will find a range of meat and fish dishes, and a lot of vegetarian recipes, which I have explored and developed while living in London and which I know you will love as much as I do. Where meat and seafood are expensive, I tend to use a few premium items – like scallops, lamb or beef – for special-occasion dishes or at the weekend. I buy the best quality I can afford and cook it less frequently.

Running a farm and a family brand (my parents have an egg farm and sell their products to supermarkets, *boulangeries,* restaurants and shops) is a lifestyle rather than a job; you can barely switch off. But throughout my childhood there was always home-cooked food on our table. Let's be honest, as a busy working mum myself, I seriously don't know how my *maman* and *mamie* did it all! My gut feeling tells me that because food had always been a priority and there were fewer distractions, very few ready meals and no delivery services, they simply did not have a choice.

But above all, when you make food a priority – for your pleasure, for your health, for the planet – then you make time for it.

Ma Cuisine
My Cuisine

French food is designed around three- to five-course meals and that is how I have devised this book. You'll find a chapter of amuse-bouches for the *Apéritif*, and *Les Entrées* for the starters my *maman* (mum) and I like to make when we have guests and for special occasions. I share with you a selection of my quick *Déjeuner* (lunch) recipes, including my famous *Oeufs Cocotte* (Baked Eggs, page 66) and many fresh French salads (pages 78–83), which are quick to prepare, nutritious and can totally be served as a dinner as well. *Les Plats* gives you a range of beautiful main courses that you can enjoy on their own, or with anything from the Side Dishes – which also includes standalone dishes like the *Gratin de Poireaux* (Cheesy Grilled Leeks, page 170). Then – *bien sûr!* – I take you right through to *Les Desserts*, which includes some of my two *mamies'* most-baked cakes: *mamie* Suzanne's *Tarte aux Pommes* (Mamie's Apple Tart, page 225) and *mamie* Gilberte's *Gâteau aux Poire et Chocolat* (Chocolate and Pear Gâteau, page 215).

We must not forget *Le Petit Déjeuner* (Breakfast), because there is nothing better than a weekend breakfast spread of dreams, including how to make your own easy *Baguette Tradition Facile* (Quick Sourdough-like Baguette, page 40) and how to master your *Sauce Hollandaise* (Hollandaise Sauce, page 25).

Chez Manon is filled with the food I love to cook, highly inspired by growing up in France, but also modernized to the conscious way I like to eat now. This book is not filled with old-school French recipes, simply because it doesn't represent the food I cook at home. That doesn't mean I don't enjoy eating those classic dishes, but I think those belong mostly in a restaurant on special occasions, hopefully coming from a chef who cares about where their products come from, too.

Finally, don't forget to have a look at my menu plans, *Host Like a French* (page 240) where I suggest some great combinations of recipes so you can create stunning food experiences and dining moments at home.

THE
FRENCH
PANTRY

The beautiful thing about French cuisine and its pantry is that most of the products it contains are widely available. Always choose the best quality you can find, in season and made locally if you can. Still, when I am lucky enough to travel to France I like to stock up on deli items like *pâtés*, *confitures*, herbs and anything that is a little more specific to where I am from.

In my Fridge

CHEESE: You'll find a lot of cheese in my fridge. I usually have Comté, grated Emmental, goats' cheese, a type of blue cheese and mozzarella.

CORNICHONS: These little French pickles are great to eat with a sandwich or some pâté.

CRÈME FRAÎCHE AND CREAM: I use crème fraîche for many of my recipes and use cream mostly for my baking.

MUSTARD: French mustard, bien sûr, most likely wholegrain as I find its taste more subtle and less powerful. I use it in vinaigrette or add to stews.

SALTED BUTTER: There is always salted butter in my fridge, ready to make a pastry for a quiche, fry some vegetables or make compôte. I usually have two types: one for baking and cooking, which is mid-range butter, and also a high-end quality butter to butter fresh or toasted bread, just because it tastes the best.

YOGURT: The simplest way to finish up a meal is to top some deliciously thick yogurt with some apricot jam (page 39).

In my Pantry

BREAD: There is always fresh bread from the boulangerie in my home in London and in France. Sandwiches made with fresh baked bread taste so much better than sliced plastic bread.

CONFITURES: Jams (jellies), mostly homemade by Maman, Mamie or me.

DELI SPREADS: Glass jars of pâté, artichoke paste and any deli spreads I can get my hands on.

FLOUR: Plain (all-purpose) wheat flour and spelt flour for baking, buckwheat flour to make galettes, cornflour (cornstarch) to thicken sauces.

GARLIC: No French cook would be without some fresh garlic.

GARLIC PASTE: In a tube.

GRAINS: Couscous, giant couscous, bulgur, quinoa, durum wheat.

HERBES DE PROVENCE: I like to bring back herbs from my trips to France and I always try to bring home some local herbs whenever we visit another country or region. Herbes de Provence usually includes a blend of rosemary, thyme, basil, oregano and savory.

HONEY: Especially to sweeten yogurt or to add to camomile tea, or a hot lemon or mint drink.

NUTS: Walnuts, hazelnuts, pumpkin seeds, ground almonds.

OILS: Olive oil (virgin for dressings and non-virgin to fry) and diverse vegetable oils (walnuts, avocado, hazelnuts) mostly for dressings.

PRUNES AND DRIED APRICOTS: I love to snack on them and add them to my recipes. The fresher, the better.

STOCK CUBES: Buy the best quality you can and keep some chicken, vegetable, beef and fish.

SALT AND PEPPER: Fleur de Sel, Maldon Salt and a mill to grind fresh peppercorns.

TOMATO PASTE: In a tube.

VINEGAR: I always keep good-quality vinegars: apple cider vinegar, red wine vinegar and balsamic vinegar to make vinaigrette.

In my Garden

HERBS: Rosemary, chives, bay leaves, oregano, mint.

le petit déjeuner

BREAKFAST

Le petit déjeuner, for me, is the meal where you can eat anything you want and in any order. You can start with something sweet, then go on to savoury and everything in between. Truth be told, I don't usually have breakfast during the week but it is my absolute must to start the weekend – cooking it for the family and eating it together. You'll find my versions of some classic French recipes in this chapter, together with some of my family's favourites. Combine your favourite recipes to create the ultimate breakfast table of your dreams!

PAIN PERDU AVEC BANANES CARAMELISÉES

French Toast with Caramelized Bananas

'Pain perdu' means 'lost bread' so this is a genuine leftovers recipe and one we used to make regularly at home. It was originally a dessert, or even a quick supper, made with the leftover bread found at the bottom of the bread basket, which would otherwise go to the animals or, only rarely, go to waste. That humble ingredient was transformed with a simple batter into some delicious caramelized and soft bread slices. I have very fond memories of making this with my dad who would always add extra sugar on top – what a treat supper it was. I now more often make it with brioche for breakfast and serve it with caramelized bananas, another of Papa's treats.

SERVES 2

2 eggs

100ml (3½fl oz/scant 1 cup) whole milk

1 tbsp double (heavy) cream

2 tsp caster (superfine) sugar

½ tsp vanilla extract

1 pinch of sea salt

4 slices of white bread or brioche

50g (2oz) salted butter

yogurt, to serve (optional)

For the caramelized bananas

25g (¾oz) salted butter

4 tbsp caster (superfine) sugar

2 bananas, sliced lengthways

In a mixing bowl, whisk together the eggs, milk, cream, sugar, vanilla extract and salt.

Heat a frying pan (skillet) over a medium heat. Dunk two slices of the bread or brioche into the egg bowl for 30 seconds. Melt half the butter in the frying pan, then add the soaked bread and fry for 2–3 minutes, until golden brown on each side. Cook the rest of the bread or brioche the same way, set aside on a plate and keep it warm.

Make the caramelized bananas in the same frying pan. Add the remaining 25g (¾oz) of butter and the sugar and cook for about 3 minutes. Then add the bananas and cook for 4 minutes until golden and caramelized.

Arrange the pain perdu on two plates and top with the caramelized bananas and a dollop of yogurt, if using.

Tip: You can flambée your bananas with some rum, Calvados or Cognac by simply adding a tablespoon of your chosen spirit to your caramelized bananas in the pan, set the alcohol alight, then leave it to burn out. Doing so adds a boost of delicious flavour.

CRÊPES

Pancakes

I'm not sure that crêpes really need any introduction but here is my family's recipe! As a true Bretonne, eating crêpes on a weekly basis is part of my identity. There are always some crêpes in *Maman*'s fridge, the ones she bought from the weekly village *marché* or the ones she or *Mamie* have made. Crêpes can be eaten at any time of the day, for dessert, *le goûter* – an afternoon snack – and even for supper.

MAKES 14 CRÊPES

250g (9oz/2 cups) plain (all-purpose) flour

4 tbsp caster (superfine) sugar

1 pinch of salt

500ml (18fl oz/2 cups) milk

50g (2oz) salted butter, melted

4 eggs

4 tbsp vegetable oil

Put the flour, sugar and salt into a large mixing bowl. Gently pour in the milk and whisk it into the flour. Add the melted butter and whisk well, then whisk in the eggs.

Cover and leave the batter to rest at room temperature for 30 minutes to 1 hour before cooking the crêpes.

Grease a crêpe pan with a little of the vegetable oil, then place it over a high heat. Using a ladle, pour some batter into the pan and tilt the pan to spread the batter thinly across the pan to make your first crêpe. Cook for 1–2 minutes on each side. Remove from the pan and repeat with the remaining batter, adding a little more oil as needed.

Eat the crêpes straight away, or keep warm while you make them all, placing a piece of baking parchment between each one. If you are reheating the crêpes, heat them with a bit of butter in the pan for the best flavour.

You can serve these with some of the chocolate sauce from the *Profiteroles Faciles* (Easy Profiteroles, page 221) and some ice cream.

Tip: Replace half the flour with wholemeal spelt flour to make thicker and slightly more nutritious crêpes that are especially loved by the little ones.

GAUFRES SUCRÉES

Sweet Waffles

SERVES 4

300ml (120fl oz/1¼ cups) milk

100g (3½oz) salted butter

250g (9oz/2 cups) plain
(all-purpose) flour

1 tsp baking powder

70g (2½oz/heaped ⅓ cup) caster
(superfine) sugar

¼ tsp sea salt

2 eggs

3 egg whites

Don't look further for another waffle recipe. I have had some lovely feedback from my previous book on this recipe and so it was a must for me to include it for you, too! *Gaufres* are so simple to make yet they make such a big impact when served – a total win for very little effort.

You will need a waffle-maker for this recipe.

In a pan over a medium heat, gently heat the milk with the butter until it has melted.

In a large mixing bowl, combine the flour, baking powder, sugar and salt, then whisk in the eggs and egg whites.

Finally, add the melted butter and milk and stir to a smooth batter.

Heat the waffle maker and, once hot, pour in enough batter to fill – there's no need to grease – and cook for 3–4 minutes until golden, then remove. Repeat until you have used all the remaining batter.

GAUFRES SALÉES BROCOLI ET COMTÉ

Savoury Waffles with Broccoli and Comté

This is a great brunch recipe, especially if you are hosting. Beautiful to present, the waffles are not only quick to make but they are also totally delicious and nutritious. I serve them with a dollop of crème fraîche and some smoked salmon, or simply with a poached egg, some halloumi and spinach.

You will need a waffle-maker for this recipe.

SERVES 4

300ml (10fl oz/1¼ cups) milk

100g (3½oz) salted butter

250g (9oz/2 cups) plain (all-purpose) flour

1 tsp baking powder

2 tsp caster (superfine) sugar

1 tsp sea salt

2 eggs

3 egg whites

100g (3½oz) Comté, grated

3 broccoli florets, finely chopped

2 tbsp salted butter, for cooking

In a pan over a medium heat, gently heat the milk with the butter until it has melted.

In a large mixing bowl, combine the flour, baking powder, sugar and salt, then whisk in the eggs and egg whites.

Add the melted butter and milk and stir to a smooth batter. Finally, add the chopped broccoli and the Comté.

Heat the waffle maker and, once hot, brush the plates with some butter, add a ladle of batter and cook for 3–4 minutes until golden brown, then remove. Repeat until you have used all the remaining batter.

Tip: You can make the batter the night before, cover and keep it in the fridge, ready to make the waffles fresh the next day.

OEUFS POCHÉS AVEC SAUCE HOLLANDAISE ET ASPERGES

Poached Eggs with Asparagus and Hollandaise Sauce

A restaurant classic, here are my tips and tricks to help you recreate this breakfast at home. You can prepare the poached egg and the hollandaise the day before, keep them in the fridge in airtight containers, then simply reheat gently in the microwave in the morning. My *maman* used to do it and I didn't realize how smart she was at the time – now I know!

SERVES 2

150g (5oz) baby asparagus

For the eggs

4 large eggs

3 tbsp white vinegar

2 slices of sourdough bread

For the hollandaise sauce

3 large egg yolks

juice of ½ a lemon

1 pinch of sea salt

¼ tsp freshly cracked black pepper

125g (4oz) salted butter, melted

Bring a pan of salted water to the boil, add the asparagus and return to the boil. Cook for 3 minutes, then drain and cool under cold water. Set aside.

To cook the poached eggs, bring some water in a pan to a gentle simmer and add the vinegar. Use a spoon to gently create a swirl in the water. Crack one egg into a small bowl, and gently lower it into the middle of the simmering water. Cook for 3–4 minutes until the white is just set. Remove from the water using a slotted spoon and set aside on top of some paper towels. Repeat with the remaining 3 eggs.

Meanwhile, to make the hollandaise sauce, put the egg yolks, lemon juice, salt and pepper in a mixing bowl and whisk vigorously for 1 minute.

Melt the butter in a pan or microwave, making sure it is nice and hot.

Whilst still whisking the egg mixture, slowly pour in the butter until the sauce blends and thickens.

Toast the sourdough bread until golden then place on two plates. Top with the asparagus and poached eggs and drizzle with the hot hollandaise sauce. Season to taste with salt and pepper.

Tips: You can also make the hollandaise in a blender, pouring the melted butter into the egg mixture in the blender goblet while the motor is running.

Keep any leftover sauce in a screw-topped jar in the fridge for up to 3 days. To serve, gently reheat it in the microwave on low power or in a small pan.

BRIOCHE AU SUCRE

Sweet Brioche

The smell of a brioche that has just come out of the oven ... I don't think there are many things in life that are better than that. I take a lot of joy from making brioche for the family, especially when they are served with *Beurre Salé Breton* (Homemade Breton Butter, page 30) and *Confiture d'Abricot de Maman* (Maman's Apricot Jam, page 39). Don't be afraid to try it – this recipe is foolproof.

MAKES A 20CM (8IN) BRIOCHE

250g (9oz/2 cups) strong bread flour, plus extra for dusting

250g (9oz/2 cups) plain (all-purpose) flour

1 tsp sea salt

8g (1 sachet) active dried yeast

140g (5oz/¾ cup) caster (superfine) sugar

5 large eggs, plus 1 beaten egg for brushing

1 tbsp orange blossom water

250g (9oz) salted butter, diced

2 tbsp pearled sugar

In the bowl of an electric mixer fitted with the dough attachment, mix the flours, salt, yeast and sugar.

In a small bowl, combine the eggs and the orange blossom water, then slowly pour it into the flour mix, with the mixer on, and stir for 8–10 minutes.

Slowly add the butter, cube by cube. Mix for another 8–10 minutes until the dough is coming away from the sides of the bowl. Leave at room temperature to rise for 2–3 hours.

Weigh out 8 balls, 100g (3½oz) each. Roll the rest of the dough on a lightly floured work surface to make a large circle about 30cm (12in) in diameter. Place the 8 balls evenly around the edge of the circle of dough. Slice an 8-branch star shape on the circle of dough, going from one side of a ball to the other side of the ball in front. This will create one triangle of dough per ball. Then fold each triangle over each ball, covering part of it. Trim the outsides of the circle to have a neat, uniform edge.

Brush the brioche with the beaten egg and leave to rise for 1 hour.

Preheat the oven to 180°C fan (200°C/400°F/gas 6) and set a bowl of water on the bottom of the oven. Bake the brioche for 25–30 minutes, or until risen and golden.

Tip: Make sure your dry yeast is still active and not passed expiration. To do this, you can add 1 teaspoon of sugar, the 8g sachet of yeast and 50ml (3 tbsp) of warm water and let it sit for 10 minutes. If it becomes foamy and creamy looking, you can add it to the brioche mix. If not, discard and buy another packet. It does take quite a while to knead your dough, so try to follow the timings given to allow the gluten to develop, creating a soft and elastic dough.

BEURRE SALÉ BRETON

Homemade Breton Butter

Nowadays, homemade butter is actually something very simple to make, but most people don't know how. My *mamie*, Suzanne, used to make hers in her wooden *baratte* back in the day, spending about an hour churning the cream from her milk cows to make her salted butter and make a few cents at the local *marché*. I make mine simply using my electric mixer and some *fleur de sel,* which makes for a very satisfying process.

MAKES 330G (11OZ) SALTED BUTTER

1 litre (34fl oz/4 cups) cold whipping cream (35% fat content)

6g *fleur de sel* (or sea salt flakes)

Pour your cold whipping cream in the bowl of your electric mixer with the whisk attachment. Start to beat at medium speed for a few minutes until the cream begins to thicken.

Continue to whip again for another few minutes. The cream is going to start to turn a little bit more yellow, meaning the cream and buttermilk are starting to separate.

Make sure you keep an eye on your mixer as the butter is going to start forming quickly. Once the butter is fully stuck inside the whisk, your butter is ready.

Line a colander with a clean muslin (cheesecloth) and set it over a bowl. Pour the contents of the mixing bowl into the colander. Use your hands to press and extract all the buttermilk from the butter. You can rinse it with water at this point, but that is not necessary.

Pour the salt into a mixing bowl and put the butter on top, then use your hands or a spatula to mix it through.

You can form a simple ball or shape it using a mould or even mini-moulds. Keep the butter in the fridge for the same time as you would for shop-bought butter.

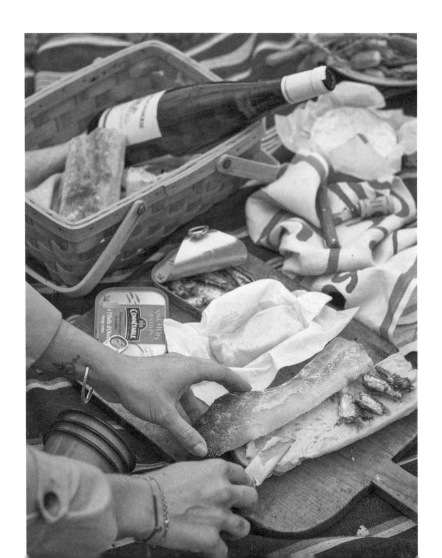

PAIN AU LAIT AUX RAISINS

Raisin Milk Bread

I had to include this recipe as it has become my daughter Fleur's favourite morning pastry. Let's be honest, she often just picks out the raisins first, making an absolute delicious mess of it! I make this version with a soft milk bread dough rather than a classic croissant dough, making it much quicker to make and something you can enjoy with the family at the weekend.

MAKES 12 MINI PAINS AU LAIT

For the pains au lait dough

250g (9oz/2 cups) strong bread flour, plus extra for dusting

20g (¾oz) caster (superfine) sugar

1 tsp clear honey

1 large egg

8g (1 sachet) active dried yeast

80ml (3fl oz/⅓ cup) milk

¼ tsp salt

50g (2oz) salted butter, diced

For the filling and crème patissière

150g (5oz/heaped 1 cup) raisins

200ml (7fl oz/scant 1 cup) milk

35g (1¼oz/scant ¼ cup) caster (superfine) sugar

2 egg yolks

2 tbsp cornflour (cornstarch)

To finish

1 egg

icing (confectioners') sugar, sifted

To make the dough, put the flour, sugar, honey, egg, yeast, milk and salt in the bowl of an electric mixer with the hook attachment and mix for 5 minutes.

Add the diced butter and mix for another 5–7 minutes until you get a smooth and elastic dough. Cover with a clean dish towel and leave to rise for 2 hours.

Meanwhile, put the raisins in a bowl of water to soak.

To make the crème pâtissière, warm the milk in a pan until hand hot. In a bowl, mix the sugar, egg yolks and cornflour to create a paste. Whisking continuously, gradually pour the warm milk into the bowl until blended, then pour the mixture back into the pan. Continue to whisk over a medium heat until the mixture thickens to the consistency of mayonnaise. Transfer to a flat container and leave to cool completely.

Roll out the dough on a lightly floured surface to a 40 × 30cm (16 × 12in) rectangle. Spread the cooled crème pâtissière on top, leaving a clear 2cm (¾in) strip along one long side. Strain the raisins, then sprinkle over the surface. Carefully roll into a log, then place in the freezer for 20 minutes.

Line a baking sheet with baking parchment. Cut the log into 1cm (½in) slices, then place them flat on the prepared baking sheet. Leave to rise for 2 hours. (I put a bowl of boiling water in my turned-off oven, and let them rise in there.)

Preheat the oven to 180°C fan (200°C/400°F/gas 6).

Brush the slices with egg and bake for 17–19 minutes until golden brown.

Decorate with icing sugar. Bon appétit!

CROISSANTS AUX PISTACHES ET AUX AMANDES

Pistachio and Almond Croissants

Croissants aux amandes were invented to reuse the unsold croissants from the day before and avoid waste. The *boulanger* would simply slice and fill them up with a frangipane and re-bake them for 15 minutes. I upgraded the classic recipe with some pistachio for even more flavours – *un delice!*

MAKES 4

4 shop-bought croissants

For the pistachio frangipane

75g (2½oz) salted butter, soft

75g (2½oz/scant ½ cup) caster (superfine) sugar

1 large egg

75g (2½oz/¾ cup) ground pistachios

25g (¾oz/¼ cup) ground almonds

1½ tbsp plain (all-purpose) flour

For the syrup

2 tbsp caster (superfine) sugar

1 tsp vanilla extract

3 tbsp water

2 tbsp chopped pistachios

2 tbsp icing (confectioners') sugar, sifted

First make the frangipane by simply whisking together the soft butter and sugar. Add the egg and mix well. Whisk in the ground pistachios, almonds and flour. Set aside.

Make a quick syrup by putting the sugar, vanilla extract and water in a small pan and heating for a couple of minutes until the sugar has dissolved. Alternatively, you can do this in the microwave.

Preheat the oven to 180°C fan (200°C/400°F/gas 6).

To assemble, slice the croissants in half lengthways. Use a brush to soak the inside of the croissants with the syrup. Then add a tablespoon of the frangipane inside each croissant, and a teaspoon of the frangipane at the top of the croissant.

Top with the chopped pistachios, then bake for 20–25 minutes until golden. Sprinkle with icing sugar to serve.

Tip: You can buy ground pistachios or simply put the shelled pistachios into a food processor and grind to a powder. You can also replace the pistachio with only ground almonds for a classic Croissants aux Amandes.

SANDWICH CROISSANT AU CHÈVRE, MIEL ET AUX NOIX

Goats' Cheese, Walnut and Honey Croissant Sandwich

This is me putting my favourite cheese flavour combination into a croissant for breakfast! I adore goats' cheese and I think the French eat quite a lot of it (France is the largest producer of goats' cheese in the world). I just love its tangy soft taste, especially when combined with a sweet, crispy croissant, walnuts and honey for brunch. It is super-quick to make for brunch with friends, served with a dressed salad.

MAKES 4

4 shop-bought croissants

2 tbsp salted butter

150g (5oz) goats' cheese
(I use a goats' cheese buche)

4 tbsp walnuts

2 tbsp good-quality honey

freshly cracked black pepper

Preheat the oven to 180°C fan (200°C/400°F/gas 6).

Slice the croissants in two, lengthways. Butter the bottom half of the croissants, then top each one with the slices of goats' cheese, a tablespoon of walnuts and a teaspoon of the honey. Replace the top halves of the croissants.

Bake for 10–15 minutes, until the goats' cheese has started to melt.

Drizzle the croissants with the remaining honey, season with pepper and serve hot.

Tip: You can also add some ham or cooked bacon on top of the goats' cheese.

CONFITURE D'ABRICOT DE MAMAN

Maman's Apricot Jam

A breakfast in my home isn't complete without a jar of homemade jam. We never buy ready-made jam in France ... and now in London, I don't either! Unlike my mum and dad – who eat one jar every two days – I keep my open jars in the fridge and they last for a very long time. My daughter Fleur loves this jam with some plain yogurt for dessert, too.

MAKES 2 X 600G (1LB 5OZ) JARS

800g (1lb 12oz) fresh apricots

400g (14oz/heaped 2 cups) caster (superfine) sugar

juice of 1 lemon

Wash and stone the apricots. Put them in a saucepan with the sugar and lemon juice. Heat gently until the sugar dissolves, then bring to a boil and simmer for 20–30 minutes.

Some white foam might form on top; use a ladle to scoop it out and discard.

Meanwhile, sterilize two jars by boiling them in a pan of water for 20 minutes. Allow to dry.

Spoon the jam into the prepared jars and seal tightly. Keep at room temperature for a few months.

BAGUETTE TRADITION FACILE

Quick Sourdough-like Baguette

My village has just 3,000 inhabitants but counts three *boulangeries,* which is probably a good average for French villages! It is fair to say my mum never really needed to spend time making too much bread, as it was so easily accessible, cheap and fresh. Now I live in London, I feel more of the need to spend time making my own bread for the family, it takes time and love, but all good things do. This version of a shaped traditional baguette, however, is as quick and easy as it gets! It is perfect for serving with your *Beurre Salé Breton* (Homemade Breton Butter, page 30) and *Confiture d'Abricot de Maman* (Maman's Apricot Jam, page 39).

MAKES 3 BAGUETTES

500g (1lb 2oz/4 cups) strong bread flour, plus extra for dusting

350g (12¼fl oz/1½ cups) warm water

100g (3½oz) sourdough starter (see tips)

3g (½ sachet) active dried yeast

2 tsp sea salt

In the bowl of an electric mixer with the hook attachment, add the flour and half the water. Mix on low speed for 3 minutes.

Add the sourdough starter, the yeast and salt and mix for 7 minutes on low speed.

Slowly add the rest of the water whilst mixing, then turn up to medium speed and mix for 2 minutes.

Transfer the dough to an airtight container and leave to rest for 1 hour. Fold the dough to stretch it 4 times, then place in the fridge to rest overnight.

The next day, gently flour your worktop, spread the dough to make a large rectangle and use a sharp knife to cut the dough into three equal parts.

For each small rectangle, fold the dough up to the middle from one side and repeat the same from the other side to shape 3 smaller long rectangles. Place on some floured baking parchment and leave to rest for 1 hour.

To shape the baguettes, gently start to roll each rectangle to elongate the dough, making sure they will fit into your oven. Pinch the ends of each baguette for a pointy end.

Preheat your oven to the highest setting, ideally 250°C fan (270°C/525°F).

Place one or two baguettes diagonally on a floured baking tray. Use a sharp knife or a razor to slice the top of the loaves diagonally, then bake for 30 minutes until crisp and golden.

LUNCH

My parents have always come back from the farm
and eaten *le déjeuner* (lunch) at home, and we
had a one-hour sit-down meal when I was a child,
so I guess that's why I feel it's important to carry
on the tradition in my everyday life in London.
Here's a collection of quick but nutritious recipes that
will keep you full until dinner. You can make them
time and again, introducing your own variations.
Oeufs Cocotte (Baked Eggs, page 66) is always
a favourite, just like my *tartines* (open sandwiches,
pages 72–73) and simple Croque Monsieur (page 54).

SALADE DE NECTARINES, BUFALA MOZZARELLA ET NOISETTES

Buffalo Mozzarella, Nectarine and Hazelnut Salad

SERVES 2

60g (2oz) fresh rocket (arugula)

2 ripe nectarines, pitted and sliced

2 large buffalo tomatoes, sliced

1 handful of radishes, sliced

2 spring onions (scallions), sliced

1 large buffalo mozzarella

2 tbsp glazed vinegar

2 tbsp virgin olive oil

1 handful of roasted hazelnuts, chopped

sea salt and freshly cracked black pepper

In the summer, when stoned fruits are at their most juicy and sweet, I love to add them to my salads. This is a very basic recipe that you can adapt and change to whatever you have in your fridge at the time.

Simply plate your rocket on a serving dish or on two individual plates, then build up your salad by adding some nectarine, buffalo tomatoes, radishes and spring onions. Top with a full buffalo mozzarella. Season with the glazed vinegar, olive oil, salt and pepper and finish with the hazelnuts.

Tip: *You can replace the nectarines with apricots or peaches. Tinned peaches will even do the trick.*

SAUMON EN PAPILLOTE AVEC LEGUMES EN JULIENNE

Salmon Parcels with Vegetable Julienne

A classic and healthy way to serve fish. I like the fact that it is quick to prepare, and because the fish is cooked together with the vegetables, it saves a lot of washing up!

SERVES 2

1 carrot

1 courgette (zucchini)

1 handful of button mushrooms

2 salmon fillets

1 tbsp olive oil

2 tbsp snipped chives

1 tsp chopped dill (fresh or dried)

juice of 1 lemon

2 tbsp crème fraîche

200g (7oz/heaped 1 cup) basmati rice

sea salt and freshly cracked black pepper

Peel the carrot, then make some thin batons, 3–4 cm (1¼–1½in) long, and do the same with the courgette. Thinly slice the mushrooms.

Preheat the oven to 180°C fan (200°C/400°F/gas 6).

Cut 2 pieces of kitchen foil large enough to make a parcel of the fish and vegetables. Place half the vegetables on each piece of foil and top with the salmon. Drizzle with olive oil, sprinkle with chives and dill, then add the lemon juice, salt and pepper. Top the salmon with a dollop of crème fraîche.

Close the foil on top of the fish, making parcels. Cook for 18–20 minutes until the vegetables are soft.

Meanwhile, place the rice, 400ml (13fl oz/generous 1½ cups) of water and ½ teaspoon of salt in a pan. Cover and bring to the boil, then remove from the heat and leave to cook, still covered.

To serve, place some rice on a plate, then carefully unpack the parcels on top and serve.

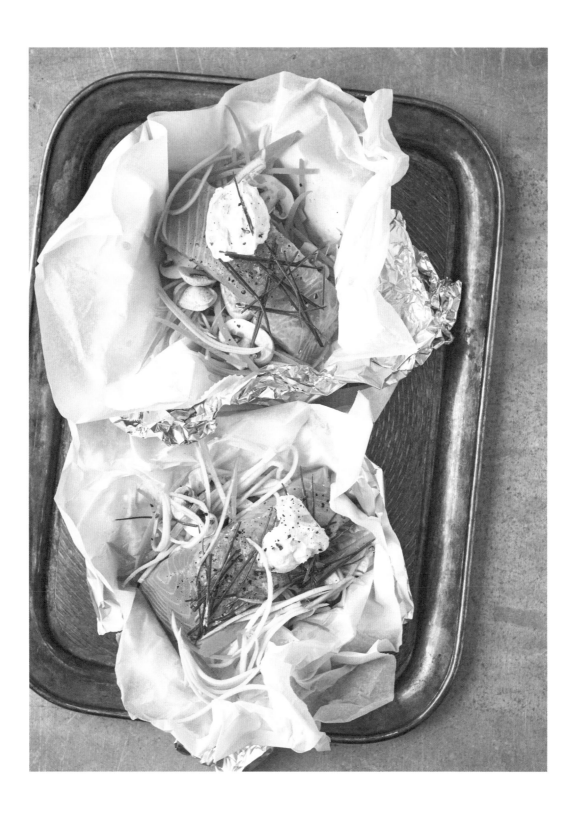

CHEESECAKE AU SAUMON

Salmon Cheesecake

This is such an easy recipe and a great one for a weekend lunch, although it serves equally well as a simple but chic starter for a meal for guests. For lunch, I would serve it with a couple of salads on the side, and as a starter for dinner, simply with a side of lemony mayonnaise. Make it the day before, so you don't even have to think about it.

You will need a loose-based 18–20cm (6–8in) cake tin.

SERVES 8–10

200g (7oz) savoury dry crackers, crushed

90g (3¾oz) butter, melted

240g (8½oz) cream cheese

300g (10½oz) soft goats' cheese

4 medium eggs

2 sprigs of dill, plus extra to garnish

2 sprigs of chives, plus extra to garnish

zest of 1 lemon and juice of ½

150g (5oz) good-quality, thick smoked salmon, roughly chopped

50g (2oz) salmon caviar, to garnish

freshly cracked black pepper

In a bowl (or in a food processor) mix the dry crackers with the butter to create a paste. Use it to line the bottom of a loose-based 18–20cm (6–8in) cake tin, then set aside.

Preheat the oven to 160°C fan (180°/350°F/gas 4).

In a bowl, whisk together the cream cheese and goats' cheese, then add the eggs, dill, chives, lemon zest and juice. Gently fold in the smoked salmon and season with pepper.

Pour the filling on top of the base in your tin and cook for 1¼ hours, or until just firm. Leave to cool down fully before placing in the fridge for at least 3 hours (or overnight).

Garnish with the salmon caviar and extra fresh herbs.

'Il y a des fleurs partout pour
qui veut bien les voir.'

'There are always flowers for those who want to see them.'
HENRI MATISSE

CROQUE MONSIEUR ET MADAME

Ham and Cheese on Toast

This is a truly comforting lunch, this little monsieur and his madame probably need no introduction! I skip the usual béchamel – which can be tricky if you are not paying attention – and simply replace it with some crème fraîche, cheese and pepper for ease, and always add a touch of wholegrain mustard – it's a real game changer!

SERVES 1

For the croque monsieur

2 slices of good-quality seeded bread

2 tbsp salted butter

2 slices of Emmental or Comté

3 slices of good-quality ham

1 tbsp wholegrain mustard

1 tbsp double (heavy) cream

2 tbsp grated Emmental or Comté

a few sprigs of chives

freshly cracked black pepper

For the croque madame

drizzle of olive oil

1 egg

Preheat the oven to 180°C fan (200°C/400°F/gas 6).

Butter the slices of bread, top one with the cheese and ham. Then spread the mustard on top of the other buttered slice and sandwich them together. Place on a sheet of baking parchment (this will make it easier to transfer from the oven to the grill).

Mix together the cream and grated cheese and spoon it on top of the croque monsieur.

Cook in the oven for 15 minutes.

Just before it finishes, preheat the grill to high, then place the dish under the grill for 3 minutes to brown.

To make a croque madame, while the sandwich is in the oven, preheat a small frying pan (skillet) to a medium heat, then add a drizzle of olive oil. Crack your egg into the pan and fry for 2 minutes until the egg white is fully cooked. Sit the fried egg on top of the croque monsieur to create a croque madame.

Tip: Serve with some cornichons and a simple salad dressed with Vinaigrette (page 186).

QUICHE AUX LÉGUMES

Vegetable Quiche

There is always a sheet of ready-made shortcrust pastry in my *maman*'s fridge for ease, but if you don't have any, the simple pastry recipe below will take just 5 minutes. This quiche is so versatile, you can really make it your own. Not much preparation is needed either, as I simply throw in my greens uncooked so that they retain their crunch. See photo on page 58.

SERVES 1

For the pastry

300g (10½oz/2½ cups) plain (all-purpose) flour, plus extra for dusting

125g (4oz) cold salted butter, diced, plus extra for greasing

100ml (3½fl oz/scant ½ cup) water

½ tsp dried rosemary

For the filling

6 large eggs

700ml (24fl oz/3 cups) double (heavy) cream

100g (3½oz) feta, diced

¼ tsp salt

¼ tsp freshly cracked black pepper

250g (9oz) a mixture of uncooked green vegetables (peas, broccoli, green beans, courgettes (zucchini), asparagus)

1 tsp wholegrain mustard

50g (2oz) Emmental or Cheddar, grated

To make the pastry, put all the pastry ingredients in a food processor and blitz on high speed for 30 seconds. If you are making it by hand, rub the butter into the flour until it resembles breadcrumbs, then add the water a little at a time until you have a smooth dough.

Remove the pastry from the bowl, make it into a ball, flatten it and place it in the fridge for 20 minutes.

Preheat the oven to 180°C fan (200°C/400°F/gas 6) and grease a 20cm (8in) tart tin. Lightly flour your worktop, roll the pastry to a 3–4mm thickness and line your tart tin with the pastry. Use your hands to line it properly onto the sides, and a knife to cut off the edge neatly. Prick with a fork, cover with baking parchment and ceramic beans (or dry rice) and blind bake for 15 minutes.

Crack the eggs into a mixing bowl, add the cream, feta, salt and pepper. Keep the grated cheese for the top.

Cube the vegetables if needs be, but I like to keep big pieces within the quiche.

Remove the pastry from the oven, discard the ceramic beans (or rice) and paper and use the back of a spoon to spread the wholegrain mustard over the base of the pastry. Spread the vegetables on top.

Pour in the quiche filling, sprinkle with the grated cheese and cook for 45–50 minutes, or until golden on top.

QUICHE LORRAINE FACILE

Easy Quiche Lorraine

Quiche Lorraine, the queen of all French quiches, is traditionally made with a béchamel sauce. I like to make mine quicker, simply using double cream and covering the base of my pastry with some wholegrain mustard. I can't tell you how delicious it tastes and it's so simple you'll make this recipe over and over! Don't hesitate to experiment; add some cooked mushrooms, some goats' cheese, some tomatoes, and serve hot or cold, with a dressed salad on the side for the perfect French *déjeuner*. See photo on page 59.

SERVES 4

For the pastry

300g (10½oz/2½ cups) plain (all-purpose) flour, plus extra for dusting

125g (4oz) cold salted butter, diced, plus extra for greasing

100ml (3½fl oz/scant ½ cup) water

For the filling

250g (9oz) bacon lardons (or 4 slices of bacon, diced)

6 large eggs

700ml (24fl oz/3 cups) double (heavy) cream

150g (5oz) Emmental or Cheddar, grated

¼ tsp sea salt

¼ tsp freshly cracked black pepper

1 tsp wholegrain mustard

To make the pastry, put all the pastry ingredients in a food processor and blitz on high speed for 30 seconds. If you are making it by hand, rub the butter into the flour until it resembles breadcrumbs, then add the water a little at a time until you have a smooth dough.

Remove the pastry from the bowl, make it into a ball, flatten it and place it in the fridge for 20 minutes.

Preheat the oven to 180°C fan (200°C/400°F/gas 6) and grease a 20cm (8in) tart tin. Roll out the pastry on a lightly floured work surface to 3–4mm thick and use to line your prepared tin. Use your hands to line it properly onto the sides, and a knife to neatly trim the edge. Prick with a fork, cover with baking parchment and ceramic beans (or dry rice) and blind bake for 15 minutes.

Meanwhile, fry the lardons in a pan until crispy, then discard the fat.

Crack the eggs into a mixing bowl and add the cream, cheese, salt and pepper. Stir in the lardons.

Remove the pastry from the oven, discard the ceramic beans (or rice) and paper, and use the back of a spoon to spread the wholegrain mustard over the base of the pastry.

Simply pour the filling on top and cook for 45–50 minutes, or until golden on top.

Tip: For ease, you can also use the best-quality shortcrust pastry from the shop.

SOUPE À L'OIGNON DE MAMIE

Mamie's French Onion Soup

It always makes me giggle when people tell me they ate onion soup in a fancy French restaurant. To me and my family, this is a dish we only eat in the early hours of the morning at the end of a big party or a wedding. It is perfect for soaking up the excess of wine consumed during the celebrations, and will help you feel better the next day. Thanks to its saltiness, water and the bread, it really does make a great secret hangover prevention. (We got through 15 litres (3¼ gallons) at my wedding!)

SERVES 6

100g (3½oz) salted butter

3 tbsp olive oil

2 red onions, thinly sliced

2 yellow onions, thinly sliced

1 tsp sugar

300ml (10fl oz/1¼ cups) white wine

1.5 litres (56fl oz/6⅔ cups) good-quality beef or vegetable stock

sea salt and freshly cracked black pepper

To serve

croûtons

Comté, grated

Melt the butter and oil in large flamepoof casserole (Dutch oven), then add the onions. Cook over a medium heat for at least 20 minutes until the onions start to colour. Add the sugar, then cook for another 5 minutes to caramelize. Season with salt and pepper.

Pour in the wine and stir the ingredients together so all the flavoursome bits are mixed in. Continue to simmer gently until the wine has reduced by half.

Add the stock, bring to a simmer, then continue to simmer gently for 45–60 minutes.

Sprinkle with croûtons and the Comté cheese to serve.

GALETTES BRETONNES

Buckwheat Savoury Pancakes

Galettes (just like our crêpes) are part of my Bretonne identity. Made with buckwheat flour, this is a dish we eat every Friday (or often on market day) in my family. It is naturally gluten free, and you can fill the gallettes with your favourite ingredients. I have included two of my favourite flavour combinations, but you'll find plenty of inspiration for your own fillings in crêperies. My ultimate lunch is to serve galettes with a salad dressed with Vinaigrette (page 186).

MAKES 12 GALETTES

340g (11½oz/2¾ cups) dark buckwheat flour

2 tsp sea salt

750ml (25fl oz/3 cups) water

1 large egg

50g (2oz) salted butter

For each galette complète

1 egg

1 slice of ham, chopped

1 handful of grated Emmental

For each galette bergère

4 slices of goats' cheese

1 handful of chestnut mushrooms

1 small handful of walnuts

1 handful of mesclun or green salad

1 tbsp honey

Put the flour and salt in a mixing bowl and make a well in the middle. Slowly add the water and use a whisk to mix it together gently until you get a smooth, uniform batter. Add the egg and mix well.

I like to cover the batter with a dish towel and leave it overnight in the fridge, but 2–3 hours would be long enough.

Heat a large, heavy-based frying pan (skillet) over medium heat for 5 minutes. Brush with a little of the butter, hold the pan and add a small ladle of batter, making a circle with the pan for the batter to evenly distribute (like a crêpe), until it covers the frying pan.

Cook on both sides for 1–2 minutes until golden. Continue making galettes until you have used all the batter, adding a little more butter between each as required.

You can make all your galettes in advance and keep them in the fridge until ready to use, or you can stuff them straight away.

To make one *galette complète*, add a teaspoon of salted butter to a hot pan. Place a galette on top, crack an egg in the middle, spread the ham around the yolk, sprinkle over the Emmental and cook for 2 minutes. Fold up the sides, creating a square with the egg yolk in the middle. Serve immediately.

To make one *galette bergère*, add a teaspoon of butter to a hot pan. Place a galette on top and sprinkle with the cheese, mushrooms and walnuts. Cook for a few minutes until the cheese begins to melt. Fold or roll up, drizzle with the honey and serve with salad.

TOMATES FARÇIES VÉGÉTARIENNES

Vegetarian Stuffed Tomatoes

I am becoming increasingly conscious about my meat consumption, and I love to create classic French recipes with a vegetarian twist. This is a take on Tomates Farçies, and I've included in the tip how to make this if you prefer. These stuffed tomatoes are so juicy and flavoursome, and represent the sunshine of the south of France. You'll find this dish in almost every bistro as a lunch special when the tomatoes are at their best. An ideal summer dish.

SERVES 4

80g (3oz/scant ½ cup) basmati rice

1 vegetable stock cube

8 large tomatoes

1 courgette (zucchini), chopped

1 red onion, chopped

3 garlic cloves, chopped

½ tsp herbes de Provence

olive oil

generous amount of salt and freshly cracked black pepper

Place the rice in a pan, then add 750ml (25fl oz/3 cups) of water and the vegetable stock cube. Bring to the boil, then simmer for 10 minutes until tender but still with a little bite.

Preheat the oven to 180°C fan (200°C/400°F/gas 6).

Slice the tops off the tomatoes and scoop out the insides into a food processor bowl. Season the tomatoes well with salt and pepper.

Add the courgette, onion, garlic and herbes de Provence to the food processor and blitz it together for a few seconds. Add the rice.

Spoon the mixture into the tomatoes. Drizzle with olive oil and a generous sprinkle of salt and pepper.

Cover with kitchen foil and cook for 30 minutes, then remove the foil and cook for a further 20 minutes.

Tip: To make the classic Tomates Farçies, reduce the basmati rice quantity to 50g (2oz/heaped ¼ cup) and add 100g (3½oz) cooked sausage meat to the filling mixture.

OEUFS COCOTTE

Baked Eggs

This recipe went viral on my socials, so I thought it deserved to be written down in order to reach even more people, because it is simply the best! I usually have these ingredients at home, making it a simple any-day lunch that takes just five minutes to prep. You will need a ramekin or a mini cocotte dish.

SERVES 1

½ tsp olive oil or butter

2 large eggs

2 tbsp crème fraîche

1 tsp wholegrain mustard

1 tbsp grated Emmental

1 tsp chopped chives (optional)

sea salt and freshly cracked
black pepper

Preheat the oven to 180°C fan (200°C/400°F/gas 6). Oil or butter the ramekin.

Crack the 2 eggs into the ramekin. Mix the crème fraîche with the mustard and cheese, then season with salt and pepper and spoon over the eggs.

Place the ramekin in a larger ovenproof dish and fill the larger dish with boiling water till it comes half way up the side of the ramekin. Cook for 15–18 minutes, depending on how you like your eggs.

Top with the chives, if using, and serve with some buttery toasted bread and a salad for a nutritious *déjeuner*.

TARTE FINE FILO À LA COURGETTE ET MOZZARELLA

Thin Filo Pastry Courgette and Mozzarella Tart

I can't resist eating courgettes when they are in season, and in this tart they are the star of the dish. The crispiness of the filo pastry is unlike anything else; pure satisfaction in every bite.

You will need a medium oven tray or Swiss roll tin.

SERVES 4–6

For the pastry

100g (3½oz) butter, melted

300g (10½oz) packet of filo pastry

For the filling

2 eggs

1 tbsp crème fraîche

100g (3½oz) Emmental, grated

3 small courgettes (zucchini)

1 tbsp olive oil

1 buffalo mozzarella

sea salt and freshly cracked black pepper

Line the oven tray with baking parchment. Use a brush to butter the paper with melted butter, then add a layer of the thin filo pastry and press it down into the tray. Brush the pastry with the butter, then repeat this with the rest of the filo pastry layers.

Preheat the oven to 180°C fan (200°C/400°F/gas 6).

Crack the eggs into a bowl, add the crème fraîche and the Emmental, and season with salt and pepper. Pour the filling on top of the filo pastry.

With a vegetable peeler, create thin strips of courgette and randomly add them on top of the tart. Season again with salt and pepper and a drizzle of olive oil.

Cook for 25 minutes, or until golden on top.

Top with torn mozzarella and serve hot with a dressed green salad.

TARTE À LA TOMATE AVEC TAPENADE

Tomato Tart with Tapenade

I hated tomatoes growing up ... now I crave them when they are not in season! Try to buy the best-quality tomatoes you can afford because it really makes all the difference for this tart. The crispy pastry is topped with extra herbes de Provence and the tapenade or tomato pesto in the base is my secret to taking it to the next level. See photo on page 71.

You will need a 24–26cm (9½–10½in) quiche tin.

SERVES 4

For the pastry

150g (5oz) salted butter

250g (9oz/2 cups) plain (all-purpose) flour, plus extra for dusting

80ml (3fl oz/⅓ cup) water

For the filling

500g (1lb 2oz) different varieties of tomatoes

2 tbsp *Tapenade aux Olives* (Olive Tapenade, page 92) or use ready made (or tomato pesto)

1 tsp herbes de Provence (mixed herbs)

1 burrata mozzarella

1 egg yolk

sea salt and freshly cracked black pepper

To make the pastry, put all the pastry ingredients in a food processor and blitz on high speed for 30 seconds. If you are making it by hand, rub the butter into the flour until it resembles breadcrumbs, then add the water a little at a time until you have a smooth dough.

Remove from the bowl, make a ball, flatten it and place it in the fridge for 20 minutes.

Slice the tomatoes lengthways and place on a large plate, season generously with salt and set aside. (This will create osmosis and help remove some of the tomato moisture.)

Preheat the oven to 180°C fan (200°C/400°F/gas 6).

Lightly flour your worktop, then roll out the pastry to a circle about 3–4mm thick. It doesn't have to be even – that adds to the charm of it.

Spread the tapenade or tomato pesto over the middle of the pastry, and top with the tomatoes, leaving at least 30mm (1¼in) of pastry uncovered round the edge. Brush the pastry with the egg yolk and sprinkle the herbes de Provence over the pastry and tomatoes.

Cook for 45–50 minutes until golden and brown on top. Serve hot and top with the whole mozzarella, a drizzle of olive oil and a generous grind of black pepper. Serve with a dressed salad.

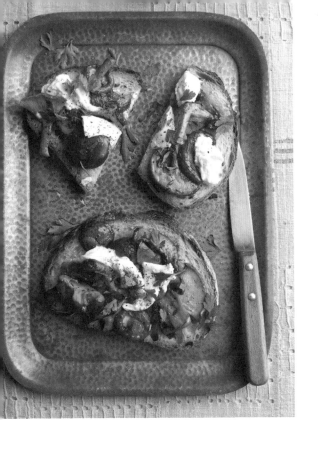

TARTINE AUX CHAMPIGNONS ET MOZZARELLA

Mushroom and Mozzarella Tartlets

A creamier tartine, I prepare my topping separately in a pan, and simply top my toasted bread with it. This autumnal tartine is great for when all the delicious mushrooms are in season, and you can use any variety available. See photo on page 71.

SERVES 1

1 garlic clove, diced

20g (¾oz) salted butter

1 sprig of thyme

3 shiitake mushrooms, quartered

6 chestnut mushrooms, sliced

2 medium slices of sourdough bread or all-grain bread

1 tbsp crème fraîche

½ buffalo mozzarella

1 tsp chopped parsley (optional)

sea salt and freshly cracked black pepper

In a frying pan (skillet), fry the garlic in the butter with the sprig of thyme over a medium heat, for 2 minutes. Add the mushrooms and cook for another 5 minutes until they are tender.

In the meantime, toast the sourdough bread in a toaster.

Add the crème fraîche to the mushroom mixture and season well with salt and pepper. Remove the thyme.

Top the slices of bread with the mushrooms and finish with torn pieces of mozzarella and the parsley, if using.

TARTINE AU BUTTERNUT, FOURME D'AMBERT ET MIEL

Butternut, Fourme d'Ambert and Honey Toast

Tartine is the French version of the Danish open sandwich. I like to adapt mine depending on the seasons, as always, and can't resist a good combination of sweet butternut with a strong cheese (like Fourne d'Ambert) topped with some honey and walnuts. Always serve it with a salad on the side and your favourite dressing. See photo on page 71.

SERVES 1

½ butternut squash

2 medium slices of sourdough bread or all-grain bread

20g (¾oz) salted butter

100g (3½oz) Fourme d'Ambert (or any blue cheese you like)

1 tbsp olive oil

1 tbsp chopped walnuts

2 tbsp clear honey

sea salt and freshly cracked black pepper

Preheat the oven to 200°C fan (220°C/425°F/gas 8).

Dice and roast the butternut with its skin for 25 minutes until soft.

Lightly toast the bread, then spread it with the butter. Spread some butternut over the bread – it should be soft enough to do so – and season with salt and pepper. Top with some Fourme d'Ambert, sprinkle with walnuts and return to the oven (or grill/broiler) for 5 minutes to melt the cheese.

Drizzle with some honey and enjoy warm.

L'OMELETTE PARFAITE

The Perfect Omelette

If you have visited the Mont Saint Michel, you might have seen the open kitchens of La Mère Poulard, famously known for its traditional omelettes. Making a good omelette is no rocket science, but it might take a little bit of practice. I like mine to be medium rare and well seasoned with a vinaigrette salad on the side – *bien sûr!*

SERVES 1–2

3 medium eggs

1 tbsp milk

¼ tsp sea salt

¼ tsp freshly cracked black pepper

15g (½oz) butter, plus extra to serve

1 tsp snipped chives

For a cheese and ham version

2 tbsp grated Comté cheese

1 slice of ham, diced

Start by preheating your small frying pan (skillet) to a medium heat.

In a bowl, whisk the eggs with the milk and the salt and pepper for a good minute.

Add the butter to the hot frying pan, then pour in all the egg mixture. Use a spatula to gently push the cooked eggs back in the middle for about 1 minute, so the uncooked egg runs to the bottom.

When they are beginning to set but still a little wet on top, add the grated Comté and the ham, if using. Once it is still a little wet on top, use a spatula to fold the omelette in two, creating a half moon.

Serve turned upside down, with some extra butter on top, the snipped chives and with a dressed green salad on the side.

RÖSTI DE POMMES DE TERRE

Potato Rosti

A *gourmand* lunch perfect for winter, rosti are traditionally from our cousins the Swiss. I serve them with a soft-boiled egg, some cornichons and a salad to make it a full lunch. They also make a simple side with a fish or meat main dish.

SERVES 2 (MAKES 4 ROSTI)

500g (1lb 2oz) potatoes

50g (2oz) salted butter, melted

1 tsp chopped parsley

1 tbsp salted butter

sea salt and freshly cracked black pepper

To serve

2 soft-boiled eggs

4 cornichons

300g (10½oz) mixed salad

3 tbsp Vinaigrette (page 186)

Peel and then grate the potatoes into a colander. Use your hands to press out as much water as you can, then place the potatoes in a bowl.

Add the melted butter and parsley to the potatoes, and season lightly with salt and pepper.

Heat a frying pan (skillet) to a medium heat and grease with a little of the butter. Press a quarter of the potatoes into a ball, then flatten it to make a rosti in the frying pan.

Cook for 5 minutes on each side, or until golden and cooked through. Repeat with the rest of the potato mix.

Serve 2 rosti each with a soft-boiled egg, cornichons and some dressed salad.

SALADE DE CHÈVRE CHAUD AVEC CONFIT D'OIGNONS

Goats' Cheese Salad with Onion Chutney

If the restaurant has a *Salade de Chèvre Chaud* (or anything with goats' cheese, to be honest) it is pretty much guaranteed that will be my choice! France is the largest producer of goats' cheese in the world and it is an integral part of our cuisine – hence my adoration for it. Its soft texture and distinctive flavour always pair so well with anything tangy or sweet, like this onion chutney. See photo overleaf.

SERVES 2

1 medium-size lettuce, washed and prepared (or 500g (1lb 2oz) mixed leaves)

2 slices of sourdough bread

3 small crottins de chavignol (or a goats' cheese buche)

a dozen walnuts

2 tbsp honey, plus extra to serve

3 tbsp Vinaigrette (page 186)

a sprig of thyme

For the onion chutney

1 large red onion, sliced

1 tbsp olive oil

1 tbsp light soft brown sugar

1 tbsp strawberry jam

Start by making the chutney. Put the onion, olive oil, brown sugar and strawberry jam in a small pan over a medium heat. Cook for 15–20 minutes until the onions are soft and golden brown.

Preheat the oven to 200°C fan (220°C/425°F/gas 8).

Slice the sourdough in 3, place on a baking tray and spread the chutney on the bread. Top each piece of bread with half of a *crottin de chavignol*, drizzle with some honey and sprinkle with thyme.

Cook for 15 minutes until the cheese is golden on top. Plate on top of some dressed salad and drizzle with some extra honey and pepper.

SALADE LYONNAISE

Lyon Salad

This salad could be renamed 'French salad' in my opinion as it is made with the most common and simple ingredients you can find in a French kitchen. See photo overleaf.

**SERVES 2 AS A MAIN
(4 AS A STARTER)**

1 whole curly lettuce (or normal lettuce)

4 eggs

200g (7oz) bacon lardons
(or diced bacon)

2 slices of crusty bread, diced

1 bunch of fresh chives, snipped

2 tbsp red vinegar

3 tbsp Vinaigrette (page 186)

Wash and prepare the salad leaves and set aside.

To make the poached eggs, fill up a medium size pan with water and bring to the boil. Reduce the heat to a gentle simmer and add the vinegar, then use a wooden spoon to swirl the water inside the pan. Crack one of the eggs into a ramekin, then gently pour it into the middle of the swirling water. Cook it for a few minutes, using the wooden spoon to keep the egg white together if necessary, until the white is just set but the yolk is still runny.

Gently remove the poached egg from the water using a slotted spoon and place on some paper towel to soak. Repeat this for the rest of the eggs.

Fry the lardons in a frying pan (skillet) until golden, then add the crusty bread to soak up the fat and crisp up for a few minutes.

To assemble, simply place the lettuce in a serving bowl (or on two plates), top with the lardons and crusty bread mixture, and 2 poached eggs each. Finish with the vinaigrette and some chopped chives.

Tip: You can keep the poached eggs in an airtight container for a night or two, and simply warm them up in the microwave for 30 seconds before serving.

SALADE LANDAISE

Salad from Landes

A true regional salad, this is filled with local produce that are easily accessible everywhere in France, but that you will probably find more particularly in French delis around the world. If you ever find yourself in France, I would urge you to get a couple of tins of confit and smoked *magret* to bring home. It's hardly surprising that my favourite pizza from my local pizzeria is made with *confit geysers* and *magret de canard*.

SERVES 2 (OR 4 AS A STARTER)

1 lettuce

200g (7oz) confit de gesiers (in a jar)

200g (7oz) smoked magret de canard

50g (2oz/⅓ cup) pine nuts, roasted

50g (2oz/½ cup) walnuts

2 slices of sourdough bread

2 tbsp fig jam

2 tbsp balsamic glaze

2 tbsp walnut oil

sea salt and freshly cracked black pepper

In a frying pan (skillet), fry the confit for a few minutes, then set aside.

Wash and pat dry the lettuce and place in a serving dish. Top with the smoked magret de canard, the confit and finally the nuts.

Season with salt and pepper and the balsamic glaze and walnut oil.

Toast the sourdough bread and spread the fig jam on top and place on top of the salad.

Tip: Traditionally, the recipe calls for the toasted bread to be topped with foie gras.

SALADE NORMANDE

Normandy Salad

Another regional cheesy salad to go with almost any main meal. Camembert needs no introduction, but have you ever tried it paired with lardons and apples fried with Calvados? You are in for a treat!

SERVES 2 (OR 4 AS A SIDE)

2 slices of sourdough bread

½ French Camembert, sliced

100g (3½oz) bacon lardons

3 apples, peeled and diced

1 tbsp butter

1 tbsp Calvados

100g (3½oz) baby spinach

1 handful of walnuts

4 tbsp Vinaigrette (page 186)

Slice the bread in half to make 4 slices, top with a slice of Camembert and some lardons. Grill the toasts for about 5 minutes, until golden on top.

In the meantime, fry the apples with the butter and Calvados for 5 minutes, until beginning to soften.

Place the baby spinach on a serving dish or individual plates, top with the cooked apples and walnuts, and drizzle with the vinaigrette.

Top with the Camembert and lardon toasts.

Tip: This is traditionally served with andouille de vire, *a smoked pork sausage, which makes a more substantial main meal. If you cannot find it, you can use any similar sausage.*

APPETIZERS

If you hear 'chin chin!' – the French 'cheers' – you
know you are just in time for an apéritif. In my family,
we generally drink alcohol with a bite to eat. It might
just be some roasted peanuts, dried fruit or crisps.
But when we are celebrating or hosting, the apéritif
is part of the meal. I have shared with you a selection
of simple, go-to appetizers from my repertoire
and my *maman's*.

'My mamie Gilberte grows pears in her garden.
She makes the most delicious Chocolate and
Pear Gâteau when they are in season (page 215).'

RILLETTES DE SAUMON

Salmon Rillettes

Maman and I make these all the time and they are always a hit. An elevated salmon rillette you can make in advance and keep in the fridge for a few days, then simply assemble or serve in a nice jar with the baguette slices and salmon on the side.

SERVES 4

1 small shallot

200g (7oz) smoked or freshly cooked salmon, cut into thin slices

a few chive stalks, plus extra to garnish

a few dill fronds

75g (2½oz) cream cheese

zest and juice of ½ lemon

¼ tsp freshly cracked black pepper

½ baguette

You can easily make this recipe with or without a food processor. Thinly dice the shallots, the smoked salmon, the chives and the dill – or blend in a food processor.

Transfer to a mixing bowl and add the cream cheese, lemon zest and juice, and the pepper. Mix well until it creates a rillette. You can keep it in an airtight jar in the fridge for a few days, if you wish.

Slice the baguette thinly and grill (broil) them using the oven grill or toaster. Either top with the salmon rillettes and garnish with chives or serve separately for guests to help themselves.

GOUGÈRES

Cheese Puffs

These little balls are just the nicest little cheesy bite for aperitifs – they are simple enough to make, but look like a fancy treat.

You could just make the gougères on their own, or replace the blue cheese top with some Aioli (page 186). This recipe follows the same process as making choux, just add cheese to the mixture.

MAKES 24 GOUGÈRES

250ml (8fl oz/1 cup) water

80g (3oz) salted butter

¼ tsp salt

150g (5oz/heaped 1¼ cups) plain (all-purpose) flour

4 medium eggs

150g (5oz) Emmental, Gruyère or Comté, grated

For the top

50g (oz) Emmental, Gruyère or Comté

2 tbsp cream cheese

Pour the water into a pan and add the butter and salt. Bring to boil, then remove from the heat.

Add the flour all in one go and use a spatula to mix it together; it will create a ball of dough. Leave the dough to steam out for about 10 minutes and for the moisture to evaporate.

Preheat the oven to 200°C fan (220°C/425°F/gas 7) and line a baking sheet with baking parchment.

Using a whisk, add the eggs one by one to the dough (you could also use a food processor for this step). Reserve a handful of the cheese and stir in the remainder.

Transfer the dough into a piping bag and cut a 1cm (½in) opening at the end. Pipe 2cm (¾in) blobs onto the prepared baking sheet and sprinkle with the reserved cheese. Cook for 25 minutes, until puffy and golden.

For the topping, mix the blue cheese with the cream cheese, then spoon into a piping bag to pipe on top of the gougères.

TAPENADE AUX OLIVES AVEC CROÛTONS AILLÉS

Olive Tapenade with Garlic Crostini

SERVES 4

280g (10oz) black or green olives

2 tbsp capers

1 small garlic clove

3 anchovy fillets

¼ tsp freshly cracked black pepper

100ml (3½fl oz/scant 1 cup) olive oil

For the garlic crostini

½ baguette, thinly sliced

1 garlic clove

If you love olives, this one's for you. Originating from the south of France in Marseille, tapenade is a delicious paste of blended olives, black or green, a touch of anchovies, capers and some olive oil. A simple dip with a fancy name, great on top of some crostini or served with some bread sticks and crudites.

To make the tapenade, put all the ingredients except the oil in the bowl of a food processor and blitz on high speed for a few seconds until it creates a paste.

With the motor running, gradually pour in the olive oil through the feed tube until you get a smooth, even paste.

To make the crostini, toast your baguette slices until golden, then rub with the garlic clove.

Serve the tapenade in a jar and spread on top of the crostini.

Tip: You can add tapenade to your quiche, or anything with tomatoes, and also make it plant-based by discarding the anchovies and replacing them with ¼ teaspoon of sea salt.

MINI CROISSANTS APÉRO, QUATRE FAÇONS

Mini Puff Pastry Croissants, Four Ways

I remember making these as a child in my parents' kitchen and now I make them in my own kitchen with my daughter. Another classic recipe in my family, loved by our many guests for decades.

MAKES ABOUT 16–18 MINI CROISSANTS

For the pastry

330g (11oz) ready-made puff pastry

1 egg yolk

For the Comté and lardon filling

100g (3½oz) Comté

100g (3½oz) cooked diced lardons (or bacon)

1 tbsp wholegrain mustard

For the Boursin and smoked salmon filling

200g (7oz) Boursin

1 tbsp crème fraîche

200g (7oz) smoked salmon

For the tapenade and sundried tomato filling

4 tbsp *Tapenade aux Olives* (Olive Tapenade, page 92) or use ready-made

100g (3½oz) sundried tomatoes, diced

Lay your puff pastry flat (keeping the baking parchment underneath), then top with your fillings, making sure to leave 1cm (¾in) on both edges of the puff pastry.

Preheat the oven to 180°C fan (200°C/400°F/gas 6) and line a baking sheet with baking parchment.

With a sharp knife or a pizza cutter, cut long, thin triangles from one side to the other, alternating at each edge to create the triangle. Brush the edges with a bit of whisked egg yolk, then roll each croissant from the longer side to the short side and seal well.

Place the croissants on the prepared baking sheet and brush with egg yolk. Cook for 20–25 minutes, until golden on top. Serve hot.

Tip: You can easily make these the day before, keep them in the fridge and reheat for 5 minutes in the oven on the day you want to serve them.

BAGUETTE SURPRISE

Stuffed Baguette

A chicer version of British garlic bread, this appetizer is always a winner in my home. It is a fun one to serve because the surprise is revealed as the baguette is sliced. My *maman* likes to have a couple of 'baguette surprises' in her freezer, so she can bake it at the last minute once guests arrive.

SERVES 6

1 long baguette

200g (7oz) cream cheese

50g (2oz) Emmental, grated

2 slices of ham, thinly diced

2 tbsp sundried tomatoes, thinly diced

½ a shallot, thinly diced

2 handfuls of chopped parsley

freshly cracked black pepper

Slice the baguette in half, making 2 small baguettes, and remove the inside using a knife or spatula.

In a mixing bowl, mix the cream cheese, Emmental, ham, sundried tomatoes and shallots. Season with pepper and three-quarters of the chopped parsley.

Use a spoon or fill up a piping bag with the filling, and stuff the inside of the 2 pieces of baguette.

Wrap the baguette in clingfilm (plastic wrap) and keep in the fridge for at least 20 minutes, or until you are ready to cook (or you could freeze it at this point).

Preheat the oven to 180°C fan (200°C/400°F/gas 6).

With a sharp bread knife, slice 1cm (½in) thick slices, making sure you don't cut to the bottom. Push the two halves together and cook for 15 minutes until golden on top.

Serve hot, sprinkled with the remaining parsley.

Tip: You can easily make this a vegetarian option by omitting the ham and substituting vegetarian cheeses.

GÂTEAU SALÉ QUATRE FAÇONS

Four-way Savoury Cake

Using a simple yet delicious savoury cake batter, this recipe offers
a choice of four seasonal fillings: olives for spring, courgettes
and feta for summer, chorizo, nut and figs for autumn, and salmon
cake for winter. The quantities here are enough for one base and
your choice of topping.

MAKES A 26CM (10½IN) LOAF / SERVES 6–8

For the base

200g (7oz) plain (all-purpose) flour,
plus extra for dusting

3 medium eggs

100ml (3½fl oz/scant ½ cup)
olive oil

100ml (3½fl oz/scant ½ cup)
warm semi-skimmed milk

1 tsp baking powder

100g (3½oz) cheese, grated

¼ tsp salt

¼ tsp freshly cracked black pepper

For the classic savoury olive cake

200g (7oz) cooked diced lardons

150g (5oz) green olives

For the summer cake with courgettes and feta

200g (7oz) courgettes (zucchini),
sliced

150g (5oz) feta

100g (3½oz) sundried tomatoes

1 handful of fresh basil

For the autumn cake

150g (5oz) chorizo, diced

150g (5oz) dried figs, halved

100g (3½oz/1 cup) walnuts

For the salmon cake

150g (5oz) smoked salmon, diced

zest and juice of 1 lemon

2 tbsp snipped chives

Preheat the oven to 180°C fan (200°C/400°F/gas 6) and butter and flour a 26cm (10½in) loaf tin.

To make the base, put the eggs in a bowl and whisk well, then add the olive oil, flour and baking powder and finish with the warm milk. Season with salt and pepper. Reserve a handful of the cheese, then add the remainder and mix.

Mix together the ingredients for your chosen filling. Add the filling to the basic batter, then pour and scrape it into the prepared tin and top with the reserved cheese.

Cook for 45 minutes, or until a skewer inserted into the middle comes out clean.

Slice into bite-sized pieces and serve as an aperitif.

les

l'entrée

STARTERS

A traditional French meal starts with an entrée,
a starter. The most traditional entrée is a small
cold dish of grated carrots with vinaigrette,
a traditional green salad or perhaps even some
charcuterie or anything cold we can find in the fridge.
I know it is hard to believe, but yes, I grew up eating
a three-course meal for lunch and dinner every day
(push it to four courses if you chose to have cheese
before dessert!). When I host, or for a special occasion,
I like to make sure we have a delicious starter. I have
selected my go-to starters here, from a *Soufflé au
Fromage* (Cheese Soufflé, page 104) to some simple
Oeufs Mimosa (French Devilled Eggs, page 116)
or an extravagant savoury Millefeuille (page 115).

SAINT JACQUES CHAUDES

Roasted Scallops with Béchamel and Vegetables

Probably one of the chicest dishes in this chapter is the Saint Jacques Chaudes. They are really easy to make, and you can prepare them the day before, then reheat in the oven when your guests arrive. *Maman* used to make this starter for big gatherings (of 15 or more people – I have a large family), more often in the winter when scallops were in season.

SERVES 4

8 fresh scallops with their corals (keep 4 shells to serve)

50g (2oz) butter

4 tbsp white wine

1 shallot, thinly sliced

1 small carrot, thinly sliced

1 small leek, thinly sliced

12 small mushrooms, sliced

sea salt and freshly cracked black pepper

For the béchamel sauce

50g (2oz) salted butter

50g (2oz/heaped ⅓ cup) plain (all-purpose) flour

500ml (27fl oz/2 cups) milk

¼ tsp freshly grated nutmeg

2 tbsp grated cheese

2 tbsp breadcrumbs

Wash the scallops well and separate out their corals (if using) and dry them well with paper towels.

Melt half the butter in a frying pan (skillet) over a medium heat and fry the scallops for a couple of minutes on each side, then add the corals and the white wine and let the wine evaporate fully. Remove the scallops from the pan and set aside.

Add the rest of the remaining butter to the pan, then add the shallot and carrot and fry for a few minutes. Add the leek and the mushrooms and continue to cook for 5 minutes until all the vegetables are al dente. Set aside with their juices.

Preheat the oven to 210°C fan (220°C/425°F/gas 9).

Use the same pan to make the béchamel. Melt the butter with the flour and stir over a low heat for a couple of minutes to make a roux. Add the milk and use a wooden spatula or a sauce whisk to mix well, making sure there are no lumps. Add the nutmeg and the cooked vegetables. Season well with salt and pepper and remove from the heat.

Reserve 4 whole scallops, then slice the rest and the coral in two, or four if they are on the larger side, and distribute evenly between the shells. Cover with the vegetable béchamel. Sprinkle with the grated cheese and then the breadcrumbs, and top with the whole scallops.

Cook in the oven for 15 minutes and serve piping hot with some fresh bread.

Tip: You could prepare the scallops the day before, cool, cover with clingfilm (plastic wrap) and keep in the fridge, ready to simply reheat in the oven when it is time to serve.

SOUFFLÉ AU FROMAGE

Cheese Soufflé

You'll mostly find this starter at a classic French restaurant or bistro rather than in people's homes. It is an old-school recipe that sounds scary to make but is actually very easy as long as you get your timing right. A fun one to serve in its cooking vessel at the table.

You will need a 20cm (8in) deep porcelain or glass soufflé dish or individual ramekins.

SERVES 4

60g (2oz) salted butter, plus extra for greasing

60g (2oz/½ cup) plain (all-purpose) flour

400ml (13fl oz/generous 1½ cups) milk

5 medium eggs, separated

150g (5oz) Comté or Cheddar

¼ tsp freshly grated nutmeg

¼ tsp freshly cracked black pepper

sea salt

Preheat the oven to 180°C fan (200°C/400°F/gas 6) and butter your soufflé dish generously.

Melt the butter in a frying pan (skillet) over a medium heat, add the flour and mix well with a wooden spoon for 1 minute. Reduce the heat to low, add the milk and continue to mix and cook for a few minutes, until slightly thickened. Set aside.

Put the egg yolks to one side. Whisk the egg whites with a pinch of salt until they form firm peaks.

Add the egg yolks to the pan, mixing well with a spatula, then add the cheese. Season with the nutmeg and pepper. (Add salt if needed, but it shouldn't really be necessary.)

Gently fold in the egg whites with a spatula, then transfer to your prepared dish, leaving about 5cm (2in) space at the top for the soufflé to rise.

Cook for 35 minutes until risen and golden. Serve straight away with a dressed green salad.

BOUCHÉES À LA REINE AUX FRUITS DE MER

Seafood Vol au Vents

My first job was working behind the counter at my village *boucherie*. The boss kindly always let me choose something for lunch to bring back home after my shift. I often went for the seafood *vols au vents*. In France you can buy the ready-made pastry cases, and they are available in some supermarkets in the UK, but don't worry, they are simple to make at home, too.

MAKES 4

For the vols au vent

330g (11oz) ready-made puff pastry

1 egg

a little flour, for dusting

For the filling

1 carrot, finely chopped

150g (5oz) small scallops

150g (5oz) mini prawns

50g (2oz) cooked mussels

20g (¾oz) butter

For the béchamel

50g (2oz) salted butter

2 tbsp plain (all-purpose) flour

cooking juice from the seafood

100–150ml (3½–5fl oz/scant ½–scant ⅔ cup) milk

grated zest of ½ lemon

sea salt and freshly cracked black pepper

Preheat the oven to 180°C fan (200°C/400°F/gas 6).

To make the vol au vents, either roll out the pastry or use a pastry sheet. Use a 10cm (4in) round serrated cutter to cut out 8 circles. Then use a 5cm (3¼in) round cookie cutter to cut the inside of 4 of the circles to create rings. This will leave you with 4 circles as the base, 4 rings to top the base and create the sides, and 4 little circles of pastry which will come to tops of your vol au vents. Brush the 4 circles for the base with some egg wash, and top them with the pastry rings. Brush the rings with the egg wash and prick the base with a fork. Brush the last 4 small circles with egg wash. Cook for 20 minutes until golden.

For the filling, melt the butter in a pan, add the carrot and fry for 5 minutes. Add the scallops, prawns and mussels and cook for 5 minutes. Drain the seafood juice into another bowl, and set aside the seafood.

To finish the béchamel, melt the butter and add the flour to make a roux, using a spatula to create a paste. Add the seafood juice and the milk to the pan, mixing continuously, and cook for 5 minutes until you have a thick sauce consistency. Finish it with the lemon zest and the pepper.

To assemble, press down the inside of the cooked vol au vents to make some space for the filling. Fill them up generously and top with the little pastry hat.

Cook in the oven for 15 minutes to make sure everything is nice and hot, and serve straight away.

'In spring, everything is in bloom and smells so good. I always think of the delicious fruits and vegetables that are about to be in season, and I can't wait to cook them!'

TARTE TATIN À LA BETTERAVE

Beetroot Tarte Tatin

An ode to beetroots, this savoury upside-down tart is an interesting and surprising starter. You could make mini individual tarts by slicing the beetroots instead of cutting them, then cover them with the pastry as described here.

You will need an 18cm (7in) tart tin or cake tin.

SERVES 6 AS A STARTER

10-15 small beetroots (beets)

50g (2oz) salted butter

1 tbsp balsamic glaze

1 tsp light soft brown sugar

330g (11oz) ready-made puff pastry

1 pomegranate, halved and seeds scraped out

2 tbsp cottage cheese

Peel and slice half the beetroots. In a small frying pan (skillet), melt the butter with the balsamic glaze and sugar, then add the beetroots. Leave to caramelize for 10–15 minutes, stirring occasionally.

Preheat the oven to 180°C fan (200°C/400°F/gas 6).

Add the caramelized beetroots to your tart tin then cover with kitchen foil. Cook for 30 minutes.

Cover the cooked beetroots with some puff pastry and tuck the pastry down into the sides of the pan and cook for another 30 minutes.

Turn the tart upside down onto a serving plate. Top with the pomegranate seeds, and serve the cottage cheese in a small bowl on the side.

AUMÔNIÈRES DE CRÊPES SALÉES

Pancake Parcels with Vegetables

A speciality from Brittany, these make such an interesting and different starter – and you can also fill them up with anything you fancy! They are super-easy to prepare the day before and serve warmed up in the oven on the day.

**SERVES 4
(MAKES 12 CRÊPES)**

2 large eggs

250ml (8fl oz/1 cup) milk

50ml (3 tbsp) water

1 tsp sugar

1 pinch of salt

1 tbsp olive oil

125g (4oz/1 cup) plain
(all-purpose) flour

butter, for cooking

For the filling

2 leeks

200g (7oz) mushrooms,
sliced or halved

1 tbsp salted butter

1 buche de chèvre

Start by making the crêpes. Crack the eggs into a bowl, then add the milk and water and whisk well. Stir in the sugar, salt, olive oil and plain flour, mixing until you get a smooth batter.

Heat up a large frying pan (or crêpière) to a medium–high heat, grease with butter and pour in a ladleful of batter, tilting the pan to let the batter spread across the pan. Cook for 2 minutes on each side until golden.

In the meantime, start to make the filling. Wash the leeks thoroughly and dice them. In another pan, melt the butter over a medium heat, add the leeks and cook for 10 minutes, or until soft. Add the mushrooms and cook for another 5 minutes. Set aside.

Preheat the oven to 180°C fan (200°C/400°F/gas 6).

To assemble your parcels, spoon 2 tablespoons of the filling into the middle of each crêpe, top with 2 slices of buche de chèvre, then close the crêpe over the top, using a cocktail stick (toothpick) to hold everything together.

Place the parcels on a baking tray and cook for 15 minutes until golden.

Tip: Serve the parcels with a vinaigrette-dressed salad on the side.

MILLEFEUILLE SALÉ AUX POIVRONS CONFITS, TAPENADE ET MOUSSE DE FÉTA

Savoury Millefeuille with Tapenade, Confit Peppers and Feta Cheese Mousse

This millefeuille smells and tastes of sunshine! I like to serve it whole and slice it for my guests at the table. It is easy to cut using a good, serrated knife. Serve with a crisp lettuce.

SERVES 6

330g (11oz) sheet of ready-made puff pastry

1 egg yolk

4 peppers (different colours)

3 tbsp olive oil

1 tsp oregano

300g (10½oz) feta

1 tbsp Greek yogurt

sea salt and freshly cracked black pepper

200g (7oz) *Tapenade aux Olives* (Olive Tapenade, page 92) or use ready-made

Preheat the oven to 180°C fan (200°C/400°F/gas 6).

Roll the puff pastry flat on a baking sheet and cut into 3 equal parts. Prick it with a fork and brush the egg yolk over the surface. Cook for 15 minutes, or until golden.

Wash and prepare the peppers, slicing each one into 4 or 6 pieces. Place flat on a large baking sheet and drizzle with 2 tablespoons of the olive oil. Season with oregano and salt. Cook for 20 minutes.

Once cooked, quickly transfer to a glass bowl, cover with a plate and leave it to steam for 10 minutes. (This step will make it easier for you to remove the skin.) Remove the skin from the peppers and set aside.

To make the whipped feta, simply add the feta, Greek yogurt and 1 tablespoon of olive oil to the bowl of a food processor and whizz for 1–2 minutes, until smooth.

To assemble the millefeuille, spread a third of the whipped feta on one sheet, top it with a third of the tapenade and finally make a layer with a third of the peppers. Repeat with the rest of the pastry and stack the layers before serving.

OEUFS MIMOSA

French Devilled Eggs

I grew up on an egg farm (which my brother has now taken over) so it's fair to say we eat a lot of eggs. A simple way to serve them as a starter is by making this recipe. The key is the addition of French mustard and chives. And it wouldn't be a 'Mimosa' egg without the egg yolk dust on top.

SERVES 4 AS A STARTER

4 large eggs

4 tsp good-quality or homemade Mayonnaise (page 190)

1 tsp French mustard

1 tsp chopped chives, plus a few chive stalks, to garnish

sea salt and freshly cracked black pepper

Bring some water and 1 teaspoon of salt to boil in a medium-size pan. Gently add the 4 eggs and simmer for 10 minutes. Remove from the hot water and cover with cold water for a couple of minutes.

Peel the eggs, then cut the top of each egg vertically, enough to be able to remove the egg yolk inside.

Keep one egg yolk to decorate the top, then mix the rest of the cooked egg yolks with the mayonnaise, mustard, and the chopped chives and season with salt and pepper.

Cut a slice off the bottom of each egg so they can stand upright, then stuff them with the egg yolk mix. Sprinkle the cooked egg yolk on top and garnish with the chive stalks.

les plats

MAIN COURSES

In this chapter, I have combined an interesting selection of *plats de résistance*. You will find a few French meat or fish classics, but mostly they are recipes cherished by my family and me. There are a few vegetarian options and tips on how to adapt the recipes (look out for the Tips at the end of the recipes). Buy the best sourced and quality meat and fish you can afford, which might mean eating it only once or twice a week — this is what I do living in London.

'Qui trop écoute la météo, passe sa vie
au bistrot.'

'Whoever listens to the weather too much spends his life at the bistro.'
BRETON PROVERB

MOULES MARINIÈRES

Mussels in White Wine

Moules frîtes en terrace by the French seaside – a true romance of my childhood! If you can get local *moules,* you have to make this dish and serve it with *Frîtes au Four* (Oven French Fries, page 166), *Baguette Tradition Facile* (Easy Sourdough-like Baguette, page 41), *Beurre Salé Breton* (Homemade Breton Butter, page 30) and Aioli (page 186)! *Vraiment la belle vie.*

SERVES 4

3 litres (100fl oz/12 cups) fresh shell-on mussels, scrubbed and bearded

100g (3½oz) salted butter

4-5 shallots, finely diced

200ml (7fl oz/scant 1 cup) dry white wine

2 tbsp chopped parsley

1 sprig of thyme

sea salt and freshly cracked black pepper

Discard any mussels that do not close when sharply tapped.

Melt the butter in a large pan, add the shallots and fry over a medium heat for about 10 minutes. Then deglaze the pan with the white wine, scraping up any shallots that have stuck to the base of the pan. Add the sprig of thyme and season with salt and pepper.

Add the mussels, cover and cook for 3–4 minutes. Then cook for another 5 minutes, using a spatula to mix the ones at the bottom back on top so everything cooks evenly. You will know they are cooked once their shells are opened. Discard any that remain closed.

Serve immediately with frîtes and bread and butter.

Tip: I like to add a tablespoon or two of crème fraîche, to make the sauce even more delicious!

SPAGHETTI AUX CREVETTES, ROSÉ ET AIL FRIT

Rosé Prawn Spaghetti with Fried Garlic

Wanting to make some quick pasta doesn't mean it should be a boring dish. The prawns and rosé combination here is exquisite, and it's a speedy way to make a delicious sauce without too much hassle.

SERVES 2

4 garlic cloves, sliced

2 tbsp olive oil

185g (6½oz) dried spaghetti

12 king prawns, fresh or from frozen

50ml (2fl oz) rosé wine

2 tsp tomato paste

2 tbsp crème fraîche

freshly grated Grana Padano

sea salt and freshly cracked black pepper

Fry the garlic with the oil in a frying pan (skillet) over a medium heat for a couple of minutes until golden. Remove from the pan and set aside.

Cook the spaghetti in boiling salted water according to the directions on the packet.

In the same frying pan, over a medium heat, add the prawns and cook for a couple of minutes. Pour in the rosé wine and deglaze the pan by scraping anything on the bottom of the pan into the sauce. Let it simmer for a few minutes until the liquid has nearly disappeared. Add a couple of tablespoons of pasta water, then add the tomato paste and crème fraîche and cook for 2 minutes. Turn the heat down.

When the spaghetti is al dente, drain well, then add it to the pan with the sauce and mix to make sure the pasta soaks up the sauce.

Serve into some pasta bowls, grate some Grana Padano on top and sprinkle with the fried garlic.

Tip: To make it vegetarian, replace the prawns with some diced button mushrooms, following the recipe in exactly the same way.

SAUMON EN CROÛTE

Salmon en Croûte

I created this recipe for my appearance on UK TV show *The Great British Bake Off*'s 'The Great New Year Bake Off 2023', and everyone loved it! I made a slightly different version for the book and tested it with my family as a celebration meal, and they really enjoyed it. It looks fancy and complicated, but it isn't. Let's impress your guests together!

SERVES 6

1 large whole salmon fillet

400g (14oz) smoked salmon

1 bunch of fresh spinach leaves

500g (1lb 2oz) ready-made shortcrust pastry

a little plain (all-purpose) flour for dusting

1 egg, lightly beaten

For the filling

1 shallot

1 bunch of dill

1 bunch of parsley

2 tbsp capers

zest and juice of 1 lemon

240g (8½oz) cream cheese

To make the filling, you can use a food processor or finely chop the shallot, dill, parsley and capers. Then add the lemon zest and its juice, then finish with the cream cheese. Set aside in the fridge.

To prepare the salmon fillet, use a sharp knife to remove the skin, cutting between the skin and the salmon as close to the skin as possible, pulling the skin aside. Slice the fillet lengthways from the middle, but only cutting to three-quarters on the inside, leaving 1–2cm (½–¾in) of fillet still attached. Set aside.

Lay some clingfilm (plastic wrap) on your worktop and shape the smoked salmon into a rectangle in the middle. Top it with the salmon fillet, opening it up to create a large rectangle.

Spread the filling on top of the salmon, then gently roll just the salmon and the filling together, and use the clingfilm to help you cover the roll neatly with the smoked salmon. Twist the clingfilm to tighten the roll. Keep in the fridge for 15 minutes.

Preheat the oven to 190°C fan (200°C/400°F/gas 6).

Flour your worktop then use a rolling pin to roll the pastry into a large rectangle 2–3mm thick. Remove the roulade from the clingfilm and place it in the middle of the pastry.

Brush some beaten egg on the pastry to help the layers to stick together, cut off the excess pastry and close the roll around the salmon roulade.

You can use some cutters to decorate your roulade with the leftover pastry, or simply use scissors to create little spikes on the surface.

Brush the pastry with the remaining beaten egg.

Cook for 20–25 minutes, or until golden.

Serve with a *Beurre Blanc* (White Butter, page 191) and the *Gratin de Poireaux* (Cheesy Grilled Leeks, page 170).

LASAGNES AVEC COURGETTES ET FETA

Vegetarian Courgette and Feta Lasagne

Another way to eat plenty of courgettes when they are in season, I love to make this dish in the summer; it is great as an al fresco main course served with salad on the side.

SERVES 4

5-6 small courgettes (zucchini)

generous amount of sea salt and freshly cracked black pepper

olive oil, for drizzling

300g (10½oz) baby spinach

200g (7oz) feta

240g (8½oz) mascarpone

grated zest of 1 lemon

300g (10½oz) lasagne sheets

50g (2oz) pine nuts

1 bunch of basil

Slice the courgettes lengthways, place in a large bowl and sprinkle over 1–2 tablespoons of salt. Use your hands to mix the salt into the courgettes, making sure they are all covered. Leave to rest for 20 minutes.

Preheat the oven to 180°C fan (190°C/370°F/gas 5).

Rinse the salt off the courgettes under cool, running water, reserve a few slices for garnish, then spread over two oven trays. Drizzle with olive oil and cook for 20 minutes.

To make the sauce, fry the spinach in a large frying pan (skillet) for 3 minutes until soft. Strain to discard the excess liquid and set the spinach aside.

In the same pan, melt the feta with the mascarpone, then add the lemon zest, season with pepper and stir the spinach back into the pan.

Start to build up the lasagne in a lasagne dish by spooning in one-third of the courgettes to make a layer, top with a layer of lasagne sheets followed by one-third of the feta sauce. Repeat to make two more layers to use the rest of the ingredients.

Top the last layer of sauce with the pine nuts, the reserved courgettes and the basil. Cover with kitchen foil and bake for 35 minutes. Remove the foil and return to the oven for another 15 minutes, or until golden on top.

TOURTE AU POULET ET PRUNEAUX

Chicken and Prune Pie

My *mamie* makes this *tourte* with rabbit (which you can, too, if you have a good butcher) but I thought I'd give you my more accessible version using chicken breasts. The rich stew paired with the sweet prunes is a match made in heaven! It always takes me back to *Mamie*'s kitchen table with my family.

SERVES 4

1½ tbsp salted butter

2 tbsp olive oil

4 chicken breasts, diced

200g (7oz) lardons (or diced smoked bacon)

1 large onion, sliced

4 carrots, sliced

4 garlic cloves, crushed

300ml (10fl oz/1¼ cups) white wine

500ml (27fl oz/2 cups) chicken stock

200g (7oz) prunes

1 tsp thyme leaves

1 tbsp cornflour (cornstarch)

sea salt and freshly cracked black pepper

330g (11oz) sheet of ready-made puff pastry

1 egg, lightly beaten

Heat the butter and oil in a large flameproof casserole dish (Dutch oven) and cook the diced chicken for 5 minutes until fully cooked through. Remove from the casserole and set aside.

To the same casserole, add the lardons, onion, carrots and garlic and cook for 10 minutes until softened. Add the wine and stir to deglaze the pan, incorporating anything that had stuck to the bottom of the pan. Bring to the boil, then cook until the wine has reduced by half.

Add the chicken stock, prunes and thyme, cover and cook over a low heat for 35–45 minutes until the meat is very tender.

Extract about 300ml (10fl oz/1¼ cups) of the cooking liquid, pour into a bowl and allow to cool for a minute or so while you mix the cornflour with a little water to make a paste. Whisk it thoroughly into the cooking liquid, then stir it back into the stew and cook for an extra 2–3 minutes until the sauce thickens, stirring continuously. Season with salt and pepper.

Meanwhile, preheat the oven to 180°C fan (200°C/400°F/gas 6).

Transfer the stew to a medium-deep oven dish, cover with the puff pastry, sealing it nicely around the dish. Brush with the beaten egg and use the knife to create a little hole in the middle to allow steam to escape. Bake for 30 minutes until golden on top.

MÉDAILLONS DE POULET D'AUTOMNE

Autumn Stuffed Chicken Breasts

Another seasonal recipe, this is a flavoursome dish that is ideal for those chilly autumn evenings. Serve it with *Purée de Pommes de Terre* (Potato Purée, page 181) and *Salade Croquante de Petit Pois et Haricots* (Green Beans with a Lemon and Basil Dressing, page 158) or steamed broccoli.

SERVES 4

1 tbsp olive oil

1 shallot, thinly diced

200g (7oz) chestnut mushrooms, finely chopped

1 tsp herbes de Provence

100g (3½oz) whole chestnuts, thinly chopped

200g (7oz) streaky bacon

2 tbsp chopped sage leaves

4 chicken breasts

To make the filling, heat the oil in a frying pan (skillet), add the shallot and cook for a few minutes, then add the chopped mushrooms and herbes de Provence and cook for 10 minutes.

Strain the excess moisture from the mushrooms through a fine colander, pressing down with a spatula to make sure you remove as much liquid as possible.

Return to the pan or a bowl, then add the chestnuts to the filling.

Meanwhile, preheat the oven to 180°C fan (200°C/400°F/gas 6).

Lay 3 slices of streaky bacon on your work surface and sprinkle with the chopped sage. Open the chicken breasts by slicing from the inside so that the chicken opens up on both sides, then lay it flat on top of the bacon.

Add 1½ tablespoons of the filling, then close the chicken breast around it. Use the streaky bacon to secure the chicken breasts, wrapping it around each one. Cook for 25–30 minutes, or until the chicken is fully cooked through and tender.

Slice the chicken breast and place on top of some potato purée and green vegetables.

POULET RÔTI

Rotisserie Chicken

The rule is simple here: you will have the best results with the best-quality chicken. I tried all my *mamie*'s tips and tricks on lower-quality chicken and it simply does not work. Buy the best-quality chicken you can afford, locally farmed and organic if you can. This is the French Sunday roast. It never gets old served with *Frites au Four* (Oven French Fries, page 166), *Gratin de Poireaux* (Cheesy Grilled Leeks, page 170) and *Salade Croquante de Petit Pois et Haricots* (Green Beans with a Lemon and Basil Dressing, page 158).

SERVES 6

1.5kg (3lb 5oz) best-quality organic chicken

2 tsp sea salt

1 tsp freshly cracked black pepper

4 sprigs of rosemary

1 bay leaf

4 yellow onions

6 garlic cloves

2 tbsp salted butter, softened

100ml (3½fl oz/scant 1 cup) water

Preheat the oven to 180°C fan (200°C/400°F/gas 6).

Season the inside of the chicken well with salt and pepper, then put a couple of sprigs of rosemary, the bay leaf, 1 onion, quartered, and 2 garlic cloves inside the chicken.

Brush the chicken with the soft butter, then season again with salt and pepper. Place the chicken in a large roasting tin.

Scatter the remaining onions, garlic and rosemary around the chicken and pour over the water. Cook the chicken for 1–1¼ hours until cooked through and tender, covering with kitchen foil if it looks like it is starting to brown too much.

ÉPAULE D'ANTENAIS OU D'AGNEAU EN CUISSON LENTE

Slow-cooked Auget Shoulder

My parents always have a few *moûtons* (sheep) running around in their fields. We let them breed naturally and raise the smalls for their meat. A 'hogget' characterizes a sheep of one or two years old, which is just as delicious as lamb and I feel it is a more 'reasonable' way to consume it. This is a simple and delicious way to cook lamb, and we usually serve it with some *Coco de Paimpol* (Paimpol Butter Beans, page 169) or green beans and *Purée de Pommes de Terre* (Potato Purée, page 181) or *Pommes Duchesse* (Piped Puréed Potatoes, page 177). The great thing with slow-cooked meat is that you can guarantee that – whether or not you are a good cook – this dish will be deliciously flavoursome and tender. You just need a little bit of patience and some good-quality meat and your oven will do the rest.

SERVES 4–6

2–2.3kg (4lb 8oz–4lb 10oz) hogget shoulder or bone-in lamb

2 whole garlic bulbs

1 orange, halved

2 tbsp salted butter at room temperature

2 tsp good sea salt

1 tsp ground black pepper

2 tbsp fennel seeds

1 tbsp thyme leaves

750ml (25fl oz/3 cups) meat stock (lamb or beef)

100ml (3½fl oz/scant 1 cup) red wine

Preheat the oven to 200°C fan (220°C/425°F/gas 7).

Bring the meat to room temperature. Place the meat in a roasting tin and start to season it. To do so, slice the garlic whole bulbs in half crossways and rub one half all over the meat. Place the remaining garlic and the orange halves in the roasting tin. Brush the lamb all over with the butter, then season with the salt, pepper, fennel seeds and the thyme.

Roast for 30 minutes until it starts to turn golden on top. Turn the oven down to 150°C fan (160°C/325°F/gas 3).

Add the stock and the red wine to the roasting tin and leave it to roast for 4 hours, uncovered, basting the meat with the juice every 40–60 minutes.

Leave to rest for about 15 minutes before serving. Use a fork to pull the meat down the bone and serve with potatoes and some green vegetables.

BURGER À LA FRANÇAISE

French-style Burger

SERVES 2

2 brioche buns

sea salt and freshly cracked black pepper

For the meat patties

300g (10½oz) good-quality minced (ground) beef

1 tbsp butter

100g (3½oz) Comté or Gruyère, grated

For the plant-based patties

½ red onion

1 tbsp olive oil

2 tomatoes, diced

½ tsp dried oregano

200g (7oz) red kidney beans (half a can), rinsed and drained, then mashed with a fork

2 tsp good-quality or homemade Mayonnaise (page 190)

100g (3½oz) breadcrumbs

For the burger sauce

2 tbsp good-quality or homemade Mayonnaise (page 190)

1 tbsp wholegrain mustard

To garnish

2 lettuce leaves

½ red onion, thinly sliced

4 cornichons, sliced

1 tomato, sliced

Sometimes, all I want is a burger – but it has to be a good burger. I like to make them for a date night, either making my own meat or plant-based patties – whichever takes my fancy. This is a French burger because it simply has a lot of key French ingredients and is served with frîtes – *bien sûr!*

To make the meat burgers, season the meat with salt and pepper and press into two 10–12cm (4–4½in) burger patties.

Heat up a frying pan (skillet) to medium–high heat, add the butter, then cook the burgers for about 2½ minutes on each side until cooked to your liking. A minute before the meat is ready, top the burgers with the grated cheese and leave to melt. Set aside.

To make the plant-based patties, in a frying pan (skillet), fry the onions in the olive oil over a medium heat for a minute, then add the tomatoes and oregano and fry for 5 minutes until softened.

Spoon the mixture into a bowl, then stir in the mashed red beans, mayonnaise and breadcrumbs. Season to taste with salt and pepper. Shape into two 10–12cm (4–4½in) burger patties.

Make the burger sauce by mixing the mayonnaise with the wholegrain mustard.

Gently toast the brioche buns, spread 1 tablespoon of the sauce on both insides of the buns, add the sliced cornichons, the lettuce, the onion and a couple of slices of tomato, top with the cooked burger and then the other half of the brioche.

Slice in half and serve straight away with some *Frîtes au Four* (Homemade French Fries, page 166) and Aïoli (page 186) or *Purée de Pommes de Terre* (Potato Purée, page 181).

BOULES DE VIANDE À LA MEDITÉRANÉENNE

Mediterranean Pork Meatballs

SERVES 4

For the meatballs

250g (9oz) minced (ground) pork

200g (7oz) minced (ground) lamb

2 tbsp breadcrumbs

2 shallots, diced

2 garlic cloves

1 tbsp herbes de Provence

1 egg

1 tbsp plain (all-purpose) flour

1 tsp sea salt

½ tsp freshly cracked black pepper

2 tsp olive oil

1 handful of chopped parsley (optional)

For the tomato sauce

a drizzle of olive oil

3 garlic cloves, chopped

¼ tsp fennel seeds

1 tbsp dried oregano

400g (14oz) can of good-quality cherry tomatoes

1 tbsp honey

½ tsp salt

½ tsp freshly cracked black pepper

My Mediterranean take on meatballs, these are served on a fennel and oregano tomato sauce. This standalone dish can accompany pasta, rice or even be served on its own as part of a spread.

Put all the meatball ingredients, except the oil, in a large bowl, then use your clean hands to mix everything together. Shape into roughly 24 even-sized meatballs.

Heat a frying pan (skillet) over medium heat, then add the olive oil and cook half the meatballs for 5 minutes, until cooked through and browned on all sides. Remove from the pan and set aside while you cook the remaining meatballs, then set aside.

Make the tomato sauce in the same pan. Add a drizzle of oil and fry the garlic for a few minutes over a low heat, then add the fennel seeds and oregano. Add the cherry tomatoes, honey, salt and pepper, then heat through, mixing the ingredients together.

Add the meatballs and their juice, cover and simmer gently over a low heat for up to 1 hour.

Sprinkle over the parsley, if using, and serve with some cooked rice and vegetables.

TARTIFLETTE

Bacon and Cheese Bake

One of the most popular winter dishes in France, *tartiflette* is a must-try if you manage to find a Roblochon cheese. This soft, cows' milk cheese from the Alps is buttery, nutty and seriously addictive. I find it is becoming increasingly readily available outside of France, but you could also replace it with Port Salut or Muenster cheese if you really can't get hold of it.

SERVES 4

1kg (2lb 4oz) floury potatoes

3 large onions, sliced

1 tsp butter

100ml (3½fl oz/scant 1 cup) white wine

1 large Roblochon (500g/1lb 2oz)

250g (9oz) smoked lardons (or smoked bacon, diced)

100ml (3½fl oz/scant 1 cup) double (heavy) cream

sea salt and freshly cracked black pepper

Peel and slice the potatoes 3–4mm thick and place in a medium-size saucepan filled with cold water along with 1 teaspoon of salt. Cover, bring to the boil, then cook for 15 minutes. Drain and set aside.

Fry the onions with the butter in a large frying pan (skillet) for about 5 minutes over a medium heat, until softened but not coloured. Add the white wine and cook until it evaporates. Remove the onions from the pan and set aside.

Fry the lardons in the same pan for 5–7 minutes until golden and crispy, then remove from the pan.

Preheat the oven to 180°C fan (200°C/400°F/gas 6).

Spread half of the onions across the base of a roasting tin, top with half of the lardons and then all the potatoes. Finish with the rest of the onions and lardons.

Slice the Roblochon lengthways, then place on top, crust-facing up. Season to taste with pepper.

Cook for 30 minutes until the Roblochon has fully melted and is golden on top. Serve with a dressed salad.

Tip: You can make a vegetarian version by replacing the lardons with cooked mushrooms and using a suitable vegetarian cheese.

PORC À L'ABRICOT ET POIS CHICHES

Pork, Apricot and Chickpea Stew

I adore apricots, especially as part of a savoury dish. They pair beautifully with pork in this summery stew, which was inspired by the Moroccan tagine my *maman* used to make when I was a child. It is very simple to prepare in the morning, to have it ready for lunch or dinner. You can use fresh apricots if they are in season, which will yield an even better result!

SERVES 4

2 tbsp olive oil

2 tbsp salted butter

600g (1lb 5oz) pork meat, diced (shoulder or leg joint)

1 large yellow onion, diced

1 tsp grated root ginger

200g (7oz) dried apricots (or fresh apricots, halved and destoned, if in season)

200ml (7fl oz/scant 1 cup) vegetable stock

200g (7oz) canned chickpeas (garbanzos), rinsed and drained

½ tsp sea salt

½ freshly cracked black pepper

4 tbsp flaked (slivered) almonds, roasted

1 handful of chopped parsley

In a medium-size pan, heat the olive oil and the butter over a medium-low heat, then cook the diced pork thoroughly for about 5 minutes. Add the onion and ginger and cook for another few minutes.

Finally, add the dried apricots, vegetable stock and chickpeas, season with salt and pepper, cover and let it simmer over a low heat for 1–1½ hours.

Sprinkle with flaked almonds and parsley, then serve hot with couscous.

Tip: If using fresh apricots, add in the final 30 minutes of simmering.

POTÉE AUX LENTILLES ET À LA SAUCISSE

French Sausage and Lentil Stew

This is my British husband's favourite stew. Comforting, with simple and accessible ingredients, it's a dish that everyone loves.

SERVES 6

1 tbsp olive oil

30g (1oz) butter

3 onions, sliced

2 carrots, diced

2 celery sticks, diced

3 garlic cloves, sliced

1 tbsp dried mixed herbs

400g (14oz) canned tomatoes

200ml (7fl oz/scant 1 cup) chicken stock

400g (14oz) cooked Puy lentils (or uncooked, rinsed - see timing)

6 grilled sausages (I use Cumberland)

Heat the olive oil and butter in a medium casserole (Dutch oven) over a medium heat. Add the onions and cook for 10 minutes until they have softened, then add the carrots, celery, garlic and mixed herbs. Fry for another 10 minutes.

In the meantime, cook the sausages using a grill (broiler) or a frying pan (skillet), until browned and thoroughly cooked.

To finish the stew, add the canned tomatoes, chicken stock, cooked lentils (or uncooked) and the cooked sausages. If using uncooked lentils, simmer for 40–45 minutes; if using cooked lentils, simmer for 30 minutes.

Tip: Serve with Purée de Pommes de Terre *(Puréed Potatoes, page 181) or* Pommes Duchesse *(Piped Puréed Potatoes, page 177).*

HACHIS PARMENTIER VÉGÉTARIEN

Vegetarian Shepherd's Pie

A French family dish *par excellance*, this is a classic gratin traditionally made with minced (ground) beef topped with potato purée. This is my vegetarian version using lentils as a substitute, but if you prefer the meat recipe, you will find the instructions in the Tip below.

For the purée

500g (1lb 2oz) floury potatoes, peeled and diced

1 tsp sea salt

125ml (4fl oz/½ cup) whole milk

50g (2oz) salted butter, cold and diced

1 egg yolk

a little butter, for greasing

sea salt and freshly cracked black pepper

For the filling

1 onion, diced

1 tbsp olive oil

4 garlic cloves, diced

150g (5oz/scant 1 cup) red lentils

2 medium carrots, diced

750ml (25fl oz/3 cups) vegetable stock

1 tsp herbes de Provence

2 tbsp tomato purée (paste)

sea salt and freshly cracked black pepper

Start by cooking the potatoes in a large pan filled with cold water and 1 teaspoon of salt. Bring to a gentle boil, cover and cook for 30 minutes until tender.

In the meantime, start the filling in another medium-size pan over a medium heat. Fry the onion in the olive oil for 5 minutes, then add the garlic and cook for another few minutes. Add the lentils, carrots, vegetable stock, herbes de Provence and tomato purée, cover and cook for 20 minutes until the lentils are soft. Check and stir a couple of times with a wooden spoon during cooking to make sure it doesn't stick to the bottom of the pan. Add extra liquid if needed.

To finish the purée, drain the potatoes, then return them to the pan with the milk, butter and egg yolk and mash using a potato masher to crush them down until smooth and creamy. Season with salt and pepper to taste.

Preheat the oven to 200°C fan (220°C/4235°F/gas 8).

Butter a medium-size oven dish, spoon in the cooked red lentils, then cover with the purée. Flatten the top with a fork and cook for 20 minutes, until golden on top. Serve piping hot with a dressed salad.

Tip: To make a classic Hachis Parmentier, simply replace the red lentils with 500g (1lb 2oz) good-quality minced beef and reduce the vegetable stock to 100ml (3½fl oz/scant ½ cup).

les Accompagnements

SIDE DISHES

Eating a seasonal and vegetable-rich diet was always a big part of the cuisine at home. You can really transform a meal with good side dishes and here are some of my favourites. Remember that you can roast most vegetables with some simple seasoning and serve them as they are or top them with one of the sauces from my sauce chapter too (see page 185). Have a look at the menu plans (page 240) to get an idea of which dishes pair well together.

SALADE CROQUANTE DE PETIT POIS ET HARICOTS

Green Beans and Peas with a Lemon and Basil Dressing

I always try to make the most of the vegetables that are in season in my cooking. Green beans and garden peas have such a lovely fresh flavour, are easy to prepare and nutritious. This side salad also makes a great lunch topped with a mozzarella and served with a slice of toasted sourdough bread. I make double the dressing and save the rest, storing it in a glass jar in the fridge. It keeps for a week.

SERVES 4

1 tsp salt

100g (3½oz) green beans, trimmed

200g (7oz) shelled fresh peas

6 radishes, sliced

2 tbsp flaked (slivered) almonds

sea salt and freshly cracked black pepper

For the lemon and basil dressing

1 garlic clove

juice of 1 lemon

1 handful of basil

3 tbsp olive oil

1 tbsp flaked (slivered) almonds

1 tsp sea salt

½ tsp freshly cracked black pepper

Bring some water to boil in a medium pan with the salt. Cook the green beans and peas together for 8 minutes. Drain.

In the meantime, make the dressing. Using a small blender, simply blitz everything together, seasoning to taste with salt and pepper.

Transfer the peas to a serving dish, top with the radishes, pour over the half of the dressing and garnish with the flaked (slivered) almonds.

CAROTTES VICHY

Vichy Carrots

A simple way to prepare carrots, the name derives from the sparkling Vichy water in which they are cooked. Vichy water contains mineral salts that give the carrots a specific taste.

SERVES 6

1kg (2lb 4oz) carrots

250ml (8fl oz/1 cup) Vichy water or other sparkling water

50g (2oz) salted butter

1 small bunch of parsley

sea salt and freshly cracked black pepper

Peel and slice the carrots with a serrated knife to about 3mm thickness.

Add to a medium-size pan, then add the sparkling water and the butter.

Bring to the boil, then turn the heat to medium–low and cover with the lid. Cook for around 30 minutes, until tender.

If there is still too much liquid, leave to cook, uncovered, until all the water has evaporated.

Season to taste, add the chopped parsley and serve hot.

u lait cru et basta !

s animaux en pâturage

u goût, du goût, du goût

e production à taille

GRATIN DAUPHINOIS

Potato Gratin

The Lagrève's family dinner often includes this dish – and usually ends in a minor dispute at the end of the meal to determine who is going to finish the last piece of creamy, cheesy potatoes. You will know why once you make it! You can slice the potatoes thinly on a mandoline, if you have one.

You will need a large gratin dish 28 × 30cm (11 × 12in).

SERVES 6–8

500ml (17fl oz/2 cups) milk

500ml (17fl oz/2 cups) single (light) cream

3 garlic cloves, crushed

2kg (4lb 8oz) potatoes, peeled and thinly sliced using a mandoline

1 tsp sea salt

½ tsp freshly cracked black pepper

150g (5oz) Comté

1 tsp butter, for greasing

In a large pan, bring the milk, cream and garlic to the boil, then reduce to a low simmer for 5 minutes for the garlic to infuse.

Add the sliced potatoes with the salt and pepper and simmer gently for 15 minutes.

Grease your dish with the butter.

Preheat the oven to 200°C fan (230°C/450°F/gas 8) and grease a gratin dish with the butter.

Remove the garlic and use a slotted spoon to gently place half of the potatoes in the dish as flat as possible and close together. Season with salt and pepper then spread half of the Comté over the top. Place the rest of the potatoes on top, season with salt and pepper, pour the milk over the potatoes and finish with the rest of the cheese.

Cover with kitchen foil and cook for 50 minutes. Remove the foil and cook for another 15 minutes to brown the top.

Leave it to cool for 15 minutes before slicing and serving.

RATATOUILLE

Ratatouille

A good ratatouille is really heaven! Hot, warm or cold, it needs to be made with love (and some time) to be exquisite. The key is to cook the vegetables in the right way so they each embrace their individual flavours before blending perfectly together.

SERVES 6

2 aubergines (eggplants)

250ml (8fl oz/1 cup) olive oil

3 courgettes (zucchini)

2 onions, diced

3 red (bell) peppers, sliced

4 garlic cloves

2 × 400g (14oz) cans of good-quality peeled tomatoes

1 bay leaf

1 tsp sugar

sea salt and freshly cracked black pepper

To prepare the aubergine, trim the ends and use a vegetable peeler to peel off half of the skin in stripes, then cut the flesh into 2cm (¾in) dice. Removing some of the skin gives the ratatouille a better texture.

In a frying pan (skillet), heat 2 tablespoons of olive oil and fry the aubergine for 10–15 minutes, until they start to soften.

In the meantime, trim the courgettes, remove the seedy part with a spoon, then dice the courgettes. In another frying pan, heat 2 tablespoons of olive oil and fry the courgettes for 5 minutes.

Once cooked, remove both the aubergines and courgettes and set aside.

Add the remaining olive oil to the first pan. Add the onions, peppers and garlic, and fry for 15 minutes until the peppers start to soften.

Add the tomatoes and gently crush them with a wooden spoon to release their juices. Simmer for 10 minutes, stirring occasionally.

Finally, add the cooked courgettes and aubergines with the bay leaf and sugar. Season generously with salt and pepper. Simmer gently, uncovered, for 1 hour, stirring occasionally, until thick.

FRÎTES AU FOUR

Oven French Fries

My *Mamie* Suzanne would often get a call from us as children to make sure she was making some frîtes before we went to her and Papi's house for dinner. I've never met anyone who doesn't love them. I make mine in the oven as I don't really have the space for a deep fat fryer, but with my tips, you will get some delicious and crispy frîtes!

SERVES 4

750g (1lb 10oz) floury potatoes

3 tbsp vegetable oil

1 tbsp sea salt

Peel the potatoes and slice them into thin French fries. Place in a large bowl, cover with hot water and leave to soak for 10 minutes.

Preheat the oven to 220°C fan (230°C/440°F/gas 9).

Drain and rinse the frîtes and pat them dry with paper towels.

Return them to the bowl with the vegetable oil and the sea salt and use your hands to mix well.

Transfer to a large roasting tin or 2 medium tins and cook for 30–35 minutes until golden, turning half way through.

COCO DE PAIMPOL

Paimpol Butter Beans

Coco de Paimpol is a variety of haricot bean that is commonly cultivated in Brittany. It has a unique flavour and mostly stays *'croquant'* – with a bite – even when cooked for hours. If you can't find them, you can simply replace them with butter (lima) beans.

SERVES 4

500g (1lb 2oz) coco de Paimpol or butter (lima) beans

1 tsp bicarbonate of soda (baking soda)

2 onions, thinly sliced

1 tbsp olive oil

250ml (9fl oz/generous 1 cup) beef stock

2 garlic cloves, crushed and diced

2 shallots, thinly sliced

300g (10½oz) fresh tomatoes (or canned)

2 carrots, diced

1 green pepper, diced

1 tsp of fresh thyme leaves, finely chopped

sea salt and freshly cracked black pepper

The night before, soak the *cocos de paimpol* in water with the bicarbonate of soda.

The next day, drain the beans and set aside. In a large pan, fry the onions in the olive oil over a medium heat for 3 minutes, until soft.

Add the stock and bring to boil. Add the garlic, shallots, tomatoes, carrots, pepper and thyme.

Drain the *cocos de paimpol*, then add to the pan and season well with salt and pepper. Add enough fresh water to ensure that the beans are fully covered in liquid. Simmer gently for 45 minutes, until tender but still retaining bite, then serve.

GRATIN DE POIREAUX

Cheesy Grilled Leeks

A simple but more gourmand way to serve leeks, that can be cooked and served straight from the dish.

SERVES 6

4–5 leeks

50g (2oz) salted butter, plus extra for greasing

50g (2oz) plain (all-purpose) flour

125ml (4fl oz/½ cup) whole milk

150ml (5fl oz/scant ⅔ cup) vegetable stock

½ tsp ground nutmeg

¼ tsp sea salt

½ tsp freshly cracked black pepper

150g (5oz) Emmental or Comté, grated

Slice the leeks in half lengthways and discard the excess of green leaves and the roots. Wash well under running water.

Boil in salted water for 15 minutes, until softened. Drain and set aside.

To make the béchamel, melt the butter with the flour, using a wooden spoon to make a soft paste or roux, and cook for 2–3 minutes over a medium heat, stirring continuously. Add half the milk and quickly mix until blended, then add the remaining milk and the stock. Cook over medium heat until the béchamel thickens to a sauce-like consistency. This can take up to 5 minutes.

Preheat the oven to 200°C fan (220°C/425°F/gas 7).

Remove the béchamel from the heat and season with the nutmeg, and salt and pepper to taste.

Butter an oven dish, place the leeks lengthways in the dish, then pour the béchamel on top. Scatter over the grated cheese, then cook for 10–15 minutes, until golden on top.

'Mamie's garden is very small, but it produces just enough leeks, shallots, lettuce, turnips, cherry tomatoes and strawberries, among other things, to delight my grandparents' tastebuds!'

ARTICHAUDS FARCIS AUX CHAMPIGNONS

Stuffed Artichokes with Mushrooms

As a child, whole artichokes served with vinaigrette was one of my favourite dinners! *Maman* would just boil the artichokes, and we'd eat each leaf one by one until we got to the holy artichoke heart. This version is better suited to a dinner party as an easy way to serve artichokes as a side dish.

SERVES 4

40g (1½oz) salted butter

4 garlic cloves, finely diced

300g (10½oz) small chestnut mushrooms, quartered

100g (3½oz) crème fraîche

2 tbsp dried breadcrumbs

400g (14oz) can of artichokes hearts (about 8) or 300g (10½oz) frozen artichokes or 300g (10½oz) baby artichokes (when in season)

2 tbsp freshly grated Parmesan

Preheat the oven to 200°C fan (230°C/450°F/gas 9).

To make the filling, heat the butter in a frying pan (skillet) over a low heat, add the garlic and fry for a few minutes. Add the mushrooms and cook for 8 minutes until soft. Use a slotted spoon to transfer to a bowl, discarding any excess water.

Add the crème fraîche and breadcrumbs to the mushrooms. Lay the artichoke bottoms in a roasting tin, fill them up with the mushroom filling and top with the Parmesan.

Cook for 15 minutes until tender.

Tip: If using baby artichokes, remove the first outside leaves, slice in two lengthways and remove the choke. Boil for 10 minutes with a squeeze of lemon, before proceeding with the rest of the recipe above.

POMMES DUCHESSE

Piped Puréed Potatoes

I remember eating these as a child – and what a treat! My *maman* didn't really have the time to make them from scratch but you can find them everywhere frozen in France. I love making them around the festive season or for special occasions.

You will need a piping bag with a large (8B) star nozzle.

SERVES 4

500g (1lb 2oz) floury potatoes

½ tsp sea salt

¼ tsp freshly cracked black pepper

4 egg yolks

50g (2oz) salted butter

Peel and place the potatoes in a large pan, cover with cold water and boil for 20-25 minutes, or until fully cooked. Use a masher to mash the potatoes until smooth.

Add the sea salt, pepper, egg yolks and butter to the mashed potatoes.

Fill up a piping bag, prepared with a big star nozzle (13-15mm) with the potato mix.

Preheat the oven to 200°C fan (230°C/450°F/gas 8) and line a baking sheet with baking parchment.

Pipe about 24 small *pommes duchesse* on the prepared baking sheet.

Bake for 10-15 minutes, or until golden.

'Opposite is a picture of my maman
and her three sisters.
We are such a tight-knit family,
even though I live in London.'

PURÉE DE TOPINAMBOURS

Jerusalem Artichoke Purée

SERVES 6

2 tbsp lemon juice

1 tbsp plain (all-purpose) flour

750g (1lb 10oz) Jerusalem artichokes, peeled and diced

2 potatoes, peeled and diced

200ml (7fl oz/scant 1 cup) double (heavy) cream

3 tbsp chopped fresh dill

sea salt and freshly cracked black pepper

The sweet, smooth taste of this purée is a great alternative to a classic potato purée. It pairs really well with red meat and also with baked white fish, simply topped with butter.

Put 2 litres (70fl oz/8 cups) of water in a large pan with the lemon juice and flour (which will help stop the artichokes from turning brown). Add the Jerusalem artichokes and potatoes, bring to the boil and simmer for 20 minutes until you can easily insert a knife into the Jerusalem artichokes.

Use a vegetable mill or a food processor to blend the vegetables to a purée. Finish the purée with the cream and dill and season with salt and pepper.

PURÉE DE POMMES DE TERRE

Potato Purée

SERVES 6

1kg (2lb 4oz) floury potatoes, peeled and diced

2 garlic cloves, crushed

1 tsp salt

250ml (8fl oz/1 cup) whole milk

100g (3½oz) salted butter, cold and diced

2 egg yolks

sea salt and freshly cracked black pepper

These delicious, buttery potatoes go with almost any dish but especially winter stews and casseroles.

Put the potatoes, garlic and salt in a large pan with 2 litres (70fl oz/8 cups) of cold water. Bring to the boil, cover, turn the heat to medium and cook for 25–30 minutes, until the potatoes are cooked through. Drain and set aside in a bowl.

Pour the milk into the empty pan, and warm it up gently. Add half the potatoes and use a potato masher to start to mash them, then add the rest of the potatoes and the butter. Mash until you get a smooth consistency.

If there is too much liquid, place the pan on medium heat and let the moisture cook out for about 5 minutes to form a puréed consistency. Remove from the heat.

Add the 2 egg yolks, combine well and season with salt and pepper.

les sauces et Condiments

SAUCES AND CONDIMENTS

A well-seasoned sauce can make any dish.
As well as elevating meat or fish, a lot of the
sauces in this chapter also pair incredibly well
with vegetables. A béarnaise on top of some
roasted carrots or asparagus makes the perfect
side dish. Many of these recipes can be made in
advance and reheated gently in a pan or in the
microwave. I am also sharing with you my 'famous'
vinaigrette dressing (overleaf), which I always
have in my fridge – and I bet you will too!

VINAIGRETTE

Vinaigrette

MAKES 6 PORTIONS

100ml (3½fl oz/scant ⅓ cup) white or red vinegar

1 tsp sea salt

½ tsp of freshly cracked black pepper

2 tbsp wholegrain mustard

300ml (10fl oz/1¼ cups) mixed vegetable oil

My house always has a jar of homemade vinaigrette in the fridge, ready to dress my salads. I think it is the only dressing you ever need. I make it in a jar directly, making it easy to keep in the fridge and pour over when needed.

Put the vinegar, salt and pepper in a screw-topped jar and put on the lid. Shake well until the salt has dissolved.

Add the mustard and the vegetable oil. Close the lid and shake it well.

This keeps forever in the fridge.

Tip: You can use half vegetable oil and half olive oil if you prefer a slightly more bitter taste.

AIOLI

Garlic Mayonnaise

**MAKES ABOUT 250ML
(9FL OZ/GENEROUS 1 CUP**

4 garlic cloves, crushed and finely chopped or grated

1 egg yolk

½ tsp sea salt

200-250ml (7-8fl oz/1 cup) olive oil

My go-to sauce to eat with frîtes and all seafood, it also pairs well with raw vegetables as a dip, or dolloped on some lettuce.

Put the garlic, egg yolk and sea salt in a bowl and start to whisk gently, by hand or with an electic whisk on slow speed.

Make the emulsion by adding 1 teaspoon of olive oil and whisking energetically, then gradually adding the olive oil a few drops at a time until you have added 200ml (7fl oz/scant 1 cup). If you feel it needs more, continue to add a little bit more oil.

Leave to sit for the garlic flavour to develop for a couple of hours before serving.

Tip: You can easily make this in a food processor – it will only take a couple of minutes.

SAUCE AU POIVRE

Pepper Sauce

SERVES 4

20g (¾oz) butter

1 shallot, thinly diced

100ml (3½fl oz/scant ½ cup) Cognac

150ml (5fl oz/scant ⅓ cup) beef stock

100ml (3½fl oz/scant ½ cup) single (light) cream

10g (2 tsp) whole peppercorns

1 tsp five-berry blend peppercorns

1 tbsp of cornflour (cornstarch)

sea salt

Sometimes, the simplest meals are the best. French food is about good ingredients, seasoned or served with good sauces. Grill a steak and serve it with this sauce and some *Frites au Four* (Homemade French Fries, page 166) for an ultimate French bistro date. You can use your own beef stock, a good-quality ready-made stock or stock cube in 150ml (5fl oz/scant ⅔ cup) boiling water.

In a small pan, melt the butter and gently cook the shallots over a medium heat for 5 minutes.

Add the Cognac to the pan and let it boil for 1 minute, deglazing the pan by stirring and scraping up anything that has stuck to the base of the pan. Add the beef stock and simmer to reduce by half.

Stir in the cream and the five-berry peppercorns. Season with extra salt if needed and cook for 3 minutes.

Reserve a few tablespoons of the sauce in a bowl and stir in the cornflour until smooth. Return it to the pan and stir well. Cook for a few extra minutes, stirring, until the sauce has thickened to a smooth sauce consistency.

MAYONNAISE

Mayonnaise

**MAKES ABOUT 250ML
(9FL OZ/GENEROUS 1 CUP)**

1 egg yolk

1 tsp white vinegar

1 tsp French mustard

225ml (7½fl oz/scant 1 cup) vegetable oil

¼ tsp sea salt

¼ tsp freshly cracked black pepper

Here is the French way to make mayonnaise, like my *Papa* always made, with a little touch of mustard! Just make sure all the ingredients are at the same room temperature before you start.

Mix the egg yolk, vinegar and mustard in a bowl, then begin to whisk with hand-held electric mixer on low speed (you can do it by hand with a whisk if you want to) and start to drizzle the oil into the bowl.

It will slowly start to emulsify. Continue to slowly add the oil, drop by drop, until it has all been incorporated.

Season to taste with salt and pepper.

Keep in an airtight container in the fridge for up to a week.

Tips: You can easily make this in a food processor within a couple of minutes.

Make an anchovy dressing by blending in 2–3 anchovies, or a fines herbes *mayonnaise by blending in a sprig each of finely chopped parsley, thyme, tarragon and chervil leaves.*

BEURRE BLANC

White Butter

SERVES 4

2 shallots, finely diced

200ml (7fl oz/scant 1 cup) white wine

100g (3½oz) cold salted butter, diced

juice of 1 lemon

½ tsp salt (optional)

Beurre blanc tastes delicious on everything!
It is simple to make as long as you keep your
heat to medium-low to ensure the butter does
not curdle.

In a small saucepan over a medium-low heat,
heat the shallots with the white wine and the lemon
juice. Heat for 2–3 minutes until the shallots start
to soften.

Add the diced butter, one by one, letting it melt
slowly and stirring regularly, until you have a
uniform, smooth sauce.

Season with salt, if needed, and you can strain the
sauce at this point to remove the shallots.

Serves warm and straight away.

*Tip: You could sweat the shallots in advance and
leave them in the pan until you are ready to finish,
and serve the* beurre blanc *at the last minute.*

SAUCE BÉARNAISE

Bearnaise Sauce

SERVES 4

100ml (3½fl oz/scant ½ cup) white vinegar

1 shallot, finely chopped

2 garlic cloves, finely chopped

2 tbsp finely chopped tarragon

1 tbsp finely chopped parsley

75g (2½oz) salted butter

2 egg yolks

This sauce never disappoints, I love it with
red meat, of course, but also on top of some
white fish with a cold ratatouille (page 164)
on the side. It's great on top of potatoes, too.

Put the vinegar, shallot, garlic and herbs in a
saucepan over a low heat and slowly bring to a
simmer, then simmer for 20 minutes to reduce.

Drain the shallot mix and reserve 1 tablespoon
of the vinegar.

Gently melt the butter over a low heat in a saucepan
and add the egg yolks, the drained shallot mix and
the reserved 1 tablespoon of vinegar. Heat through,
allowing it to thicken but not to boil.

Serve immediately, or leave to cool and reheat
in a bain marie, stirring continuously.

SAUCE À L'ESTRAGON

Tarragon Sauce

MAKES ABOUT 240ML (7 1/2FL OZ/1 CUP)

20g (¾oz) salted butter

2 shallots, thinly diced

20g (¾oz) tarragon leaves, chopped

200g (7oz/scant 1 cup) créme fraîche

½ tsp salt

¼ tsp freshly cracked black pepper

The perfect sauce for fish or white meat and to top some roasted vegetables.

Melt the butter in a saucepan, add the shallots and cook over a medium heat for 5 minutes until the shallots are softened.

Add the tarragon and the crème fraîche, season with salt and pepper and simmer gently for 10 minutes, stirring occasionally.

Serve hot or cooled.

SAUCE AUX ÉCHALOTTES

Shallot Sauce

SERVES 4

10 shallots (about 150g/5oz), thinly sliced

50g (2oz) salted butter

1 tsp sugar

250ml (9fl oz/generous 1 cup) red wine

½ tsp salt

½ tsp freshly cracked black pepper

My uncle has served this dish for decades in his restaurant 'Le Bretagne'. I think it is my favourite sauce to serve with beef.

Melt the butter over a medium heat and add the shallots. Cook for 5 minutes, stirring gently with a wooden spoon, until the shallots start to soften.

Sprinkle the sugar over the top, then continue to heat and stir gently for another 5 minutes until the shallots caramelize.

Pour over the wine, season with salt and pepper and bring to the boil.

Turn the heat to low, cover and cook for 15–20 minutes, or until the liquid has almost evaporated.

Serve warm.

Tip: You can make this the day before, keep it in an airtight container and reheat in a saucepan just before serving.

1kg

3,50 €   soit le kg

€

Produit ECHALOTES

Variété de consommation rond

Origine FRANCE

Calibre 32/55

Catégorie

BLANC 11,00 €/100g   1129   110€/kg

TRAPPEUR 10,80 €/100g   1304   108€/kg

POIVRE KAMP NOIR 12,00   1110   120

5 BAIES 10,00 €/100   1115

49,50€/KG

POIVRE PEN

les
fromages

CHEESEBOARD

Les Fromages is traditionally served between *le plat* and *le dessert*. In my house there is always a Camembert or a local cheese in the fridge for everyday consumption. The cheeses are kept in an airtight cheese container to avoid making all the other foods in the fridge smell of it!

L'ART DE CRÉER UN PLATEAU DE FROMAGE

The Art of the Cheeseboard

For a family meal, we may have one or two cheeses but when we have guests, we prepare a proper *plateau de fromage*. Here are a few of my tips to create your best version at home.

- **Preparation**

Prepare the cheeseboard before your guests arrive and keep it in a cool room but outside of the fridge. Most cheeses will taste their best and be easier to cut when eaten at room temperature. If you don't have a cool room, prepare the platter, cover it and keep it in the fridge, then remove it 30 minutes before serving it.

Invest in a nice wooden cheese platter and a couple of cheese knives. I personally prefer the texture of the wood for the board, but a granite or marble one will keep your cheeses at the correct temperature. Get one with a glass cover for something even more impressive to bring to the table; it will enhance the joy of serving your cheeses. Don't forget to add a spoon for any liquid cheeses, and to make sure the soft cheeses (like Roquefort) have their own knife.

My *maman* always made sure a piece of each cheese was cut out before serving a platter. This makes it easier for the guests to serve themselves and also for them to check the texture inside the cheeses.

- **How Many Cheeses?**

How many different cheeses makes up a good cheeseboard? I usually choose five different cheeses, especially when served between the main course and dessert, when I allow 70-90g (2½-3¼oz) of cheese per person. If served at the end of a meal or after dessert, I allow up to 120g (4oz) as people tend to eat more of it then. But overall, think quality rather than quantity. Sometimes, a platter with only three good farm cheeses is best!

- **The Selection**

To create the perfect selection, you'll want a variety of textures, types of milk and flavours. Here are some examples of my favourites.

An uncooked pressed cheese: Mostly like a mountain cheese, such as Cantal, Morbier, Tomme de Savoie, mimolette, Gouda Vieux
A cooked pressed cheese: Comté, Beaufort, Gruyère, Emmental
A soft cheese with a bloomy rind: Brie, Camembert, Neufchatel
A soft cheese with a washed rind: Pont l'Evêque, Tête de Moine
You can add a goats' milk cheese: Buche de Chèvre or Crotin de Chavignol
A blue cheese: Roquefort, Fourme d'Ambert, Gorgonzola, Stilton

- **How to Serve**

For the purists, the only additional items on the *plateau de fromage* would be a few grapes, and some dressed lettuce and fresh bread on the side. I have learnt to love my cheeses with fig jam, black cherry jam, salted almonds and figs.

The correct order to eat your cheese will be from the milder in taste to the strongest, so that is also the order you should place your cheeses on the platter. Making sure you cut and clean your palate with a sip of wine or a grape between cheeses.

les desserts

DESSERTS

No meal is complete without something sweet in my home (in France or in England!). Sometimes it is plain yogurt with homemade *Confiture d'Abricot de Maman* (Maman's Apricot Jam, page 39), a piece of bread and confiture or, naturally, a slice of cake. My first book, *Et Voilà!*, includes all my ultimate 80 French desserts but I couldn't end *Chez Manon* without a selection of puddings.

'Happiness, to me, is sharing a dessert with my husband every single night after dinner on the sofa.'

FLAN PARISIEN

Parisian Flan

You'll find this flan in most *boulangeries* around France – not only in Paris! The thick and smooth custardy filling encased with flaky pastry is also very easy to make at home.

You will need a 22–25cm (9–9½in) loose-based cake tin.

SERVES 4

For the filling

700ml (24fl oz/3 cups) whole milk

250g (9oz/heaped 1 cup) caster (superfine) sugar

1 tbsp vanilla paste (or 1 whole vanilla pod or 1 tsp vanilla extract)

4 egg yolks

1 large egg

90g (3½oz/scant 1 cup) cornflour (cornstarch)

For the pastry (or use shop-bought shortcrust pastry)

125g (4½oz) salted butter, at room temperature

150g (5oz/scant 1¼ cups) plain (all-purpose) flour, plus extra for dusting

1 tbsp caster (superfine) sugar

1 egg

3 tbsp cold water

If you are making the pastry, do this first. In a bowl, mix together the butter and flour with your fingertips until it resembles breadcrumbs. Add the egg and continue mixing with your hands until well combined. Tip the mix out of the bowl onto a clean benchtop and shape to a round. Add the water and combine the mixture until it forms a compact ball. Wrap in clingfilm (plastic wrap) and transfer to the fridge for 15 minutes before using.

To make the filling, in a saucepan, bring the milk to boil with the sugar and the vanilla and set aside.

In a bowl, mix the egg yolks with the egg and the cornflour.

Pour the warm milk over the egg mixture, then return to the pan. Use a wooden spoon to stir constantly while cooking over a medium heat for 4–5 minutes, or until the sauce is thick enough to coat the back of the spoon. Cover and set aside.

Flour your benchtop and use a rolling pin to create a circle of pastry, about 3–4 mm thick. Use the pastry to line your tin, prick the base with a fork and place in the freezer for 15 minutes.

Preheat the oven to 200°C fan (220°C/425°F/gas 8).

Pour the flan filling into the pastry case and cook for 40–45 minutes, or until just set.

Leave to cool completely before placing the flan in the fridge for at least 5 hours before slicing and serving.

TARTE TATIN AUX ABRICOTS ET À LA FRANGIPANE

Apricots and Frangipane Tarte Tatin

When apricots are in season, it is my fruit of choice to bake with. Juicy, caramelized apricots on top of a buttery almond frangipane, the queen tart for your al fresco summer meals.

You will need an 18cm (7½in) tart tin.

SERVES 4–6

500g (1lb 2oz) apricots

25g (¾oz) butter

2 tbsp brown sugar

For the Frangipane

100g (3½oz) salted butter at room temperature

100g (3½oz/heaped ½ cup) light soft brown sugar

100g (3½oz/1 cup) ground almonds

30g (1oz/¼ cup) plain (all-purpose) flour

1 tsp vanilla extract

1 large egg

1 sheet (330g /11oz) of shop-bought puff pastry

To serve

crème fraîche

Preheat the oven to 180°C fan (200°C/400°F/gas 6) and line a 20cm (8in) cake tin with baking parchment.

Roast the apricots for 30 minutes with the butter and the brown sugar.

In the meantime, make the frangipane by mixing the soft butter with the brown sugar, ground almonds and flour, vanilla extract and the egg.

Arrange the roasted apricots in the prepared tin. Fill a piping bag with a large nozzle with the frangipane and pipe the frangipane on top of the apricots.

Cover the frangipane with the puff pastry and fold the pastry round the edges, tucking it down the sides to seal. Use a knife to make a small cut in the middle of the pastry lid so the steam can escape.

Bake for 40–45 minutes until golden. Turn upside-down straight away and serve with crème fraîche.

TARTE TROPÉZIENNE

Saint-Tropez Tart

SERVES 6

For the brioche

250g (9oz/2 cups) strong bread flour

250g (9oz/2 cup) plain (all-purpose) flour

100g (3½oz/heaped 1 cup) sugar

1 tsp sea salt

8g (1 sachet) active dried yeast

7 large eggs

1½ tsp orange blossom

scant 3 tbsp milk

250g (9oz) salted butter, diced, plus extra for greasing

2 tbsp pearled or nibbed sugar

For the crème patissière

250ml (9fl oz/2 cups) whole milk

1 tbsp vanilla paste or 2 fresh vanilla pods, seeds scraped out

3 egg yolks

40g (1½oz/scant ⅓ cup) plain (all-purpose) flour, plus extra for dusting

100g (3½oz/scant ⅔ cup) caster (superfine) sugar

200ml (7fl oz/scant 1 cup) double (heavy) cream

Made popular in the 1950s by Brigitte Bardot in Saint-Tropez, this brioche with pearl sugar filled with crème patissière is simply divine and decadent! It makes a super centrepiece for a garden party dessert in the summer, and the leftovers make a delicious *goûter* for the little ones. If you don't have pearled sugar, you can use Demerara instead.

You will need a 24cm (9½in) loose-based cake tin.

First, make the brioche. In the bowl of an electric mixer with the dough attachment, mix the flours, sugar, salt and yeast. In another bowl, mix 6 eggs and the orange blossom. Slowly add the egg mixture to the flour bowl, with the machine mixing, then mix for 8–10 minutes, adding the milk if the dough is too stiff.

Slowly add the butter, cube by cube. Mix for another 8–10 minutes, until the dough doesn't stick to the bowl any more. Form into a ball, cover, and leave to rise for 2–3 hours in a warm place.

In the meantime, make the crème patissière. Warm up the milk with the vanilla paste or the vanilla seeds and pods in a heavy-based pan over a medium heat.

In a glass bowl, mix the egg yolks with the flour and sugar. Pour half of the warm milk over the egg yolk mix and whisk well, then pour over the rest of the milk and return the mixture to the pan. Cook for a few minutes until the crème patissière is quite thick, stirring continuously.

Return the patissière to the bowl to cool down, cover with clingfilm (plastic wrap) or a food-safe cover.

Now the brioche has doubled in size, remove the air from the dough by kneading it on a benchtop, then shape into a large ball. Grease the cake tin with butter, then place the brioche in the middle and push to the sides to fill up the tin.

Beat the last egg and use the egg wash to brush over the brioche and leave it to rise for another hour or two.

Preheat the oven to 180°C fan (200°C/400°F/gas 6).

Brush some more egg wash over the brioche, sprinkle with the pearl sugar and bake for 35–40 minutes, until golden and thoroughly cooked.

To finish the crème patissière, whip the cream to soft peaks. Use a spatula to loosen up the crème patissière, then add the whipped cream to it and softly incorporate it into the cream. Transfer to a piping bag.

Once the brioche is done, allow it to cool completely, then slice it in half. Pipe the crème patissière on the bottom half of the brioche and then put the other half on top.

Tip: You can also add some fruit compôte, jam or even some fresh fruit.

GÂTEAUX AUX POIRES ET CHOCOLAT

Chocolate and Pear Gâteau

Mamie Gilberte grows the most delicious Conference pears in her garden, and this is her simple French cake recipe with pear and chocolate. It is a moist and totally moreish cake that you can enjoy warm or cold. *Merci, Mamie!*

SERVES 6

240g (8½oz/scant 2 cups) plain (all-purpose) flour

220g (8oz/scant 1¼ cups) caster (superfine) sugar

1 tsp baking powder

1 pinch of salt

80g (3oz) salted butter, diced

240ml (8fl oz/scant 1 cup) whole milk

2 large eggs

1 tsp vanilla paste

100g (3½oz) dark chocolate, roughly chopped

4 pears, peeled and cored, then 2 diced and 2 sliced

Preheat the oven to 180°C fan (200°C/400°F/gas 6) and grease and line a 20cm (8in) cake tin.

In a mixing bowl, add the flour, sugar, baking powder, pinch of salt and the diced butter. Use your hands to crumble the butter into the rest of the dried ingredients until you get a fine crumbled texture. (You could also use a food processor.)

In another mixing bowl, mix the milk, eggs and vanilla paste. Add this to the crumble mixture and blend to create a uniform batter.

Reserve a spoonful of the chocolate for decoration, then add the rest to the bowl with the diced pears. Spoon into the prepared tin, arrange the sliced pears on top and sprinkle with the reserved chocolate.

Bake for 40–45 minutes, or until golden on top. You can cover the top with kitchen foil half way through the bake if it appears to be browning too much.

ÎLES FLOTTANTES

Floating Islands

My uncle used to make this dessert in his restaurant, 'Le Bretagne', and I have so many fond memories of the sweet and soft poached egg whites with the crème anglaise and the sweet caramel and flaked almonds on top! It is not particularly a dessert we made in my home (since we had it at my uncle's!) but it makes a perfect light dessert to end a meal.

You will need a large oven tray and an 18–20cm (7–8in) round cake tin that sits comfortably inside the oven tray to make a bain marie.

SERVES 4

For the caramel

200g (7oz/heaped 1 cup) caster (superfine) sugar

For the islands

4 large egg whites

¼ tsp sea salt

75 g (2½oz/heaped ½ cup) icing (confectioners') sugar, sifted

For the crème anglaise

500ml (17fl oz/2 cups) whole milk

4 egg yolks

1 tbsp vanilla paste or 2 vanilla pods, seeds scraped out

75g (2½oz/scant ½ cup) caster (superfine) sugar

2 tbsp roasted flaked (slivered) almonds

To make the caramel, place the caster sugar and 3 tablespoons of water in a heavy-based pan and leave over a low heat to cook for 5–10 minutes, until the caramel gets a nice brown caramel colour. Keep a close watch on it as it will turn fairly suddenly. Set aside.

To make the islands, whip the egg whites with the salt until it forms soft peaks. Increase the speed and add the icing sugar a spoonful at a time, then continue to whisk until it forms firm peaks.

Preheat the oven to 120°C fan (140°C/275°F/gas 3).

Spoon half the caramel into the cake tin, then spoon the whipped egg white on top using a spatula. Place the cake tin inside the large oven tray and fill the tray with boiling water to come half way up the sides of the tin. Cook the eggs for 30 minutes.

Meanwhile, make the crème anglaise. Warm the milk with the vanilla pods in a heavy-based pan over a low heat. In a bowl, whisk the egg yolks with the sugar until the mixture turns pale. Add half of the warmed milk to the mixture and mix well, then return this to the pan.

Cook on medium-low heat for 10 minutes, mixing with a wooden spoon, until you have a thicker sauce consistency.

Pour the crème anglaise into a deep serving dish, place the cooked egg whites on top with the caramel (so they float). Drizzle with some extra caramel and finish with the almonds.

MOUSSE AU CHOCOLAT BLANC ET FRUITS DE LA PASSION

White Chocolate Mousse with Passion Fruit Curd

The tangy and tartness of the passion fruit curd cuts deep with the white chocolate sweetness. I adore this flavour combination and it is a dessert you can prepare a couple of days before with little preparation needed.

SERVES 4

150g (5oz) white chocolate

200ml (7fl oz/scant 1 cup) double (heavy) cream

3 large eggs, separated

1 tbsp caster (superfine) sugar

6 passion fruits, seeds scraped out, plus extra to garnish (optional)

1 pinch of sea salt

50g (2oz/scant ⅓ cup) caster (superfine) sugar

a little grated coconut, to garnish

Melt the chocolate and cream in a heatproof bowl set over a pan of gently simmering water (or in a microwave, at 30 second intervals). Leave it to cool until room temperature.

Meanwhile, make the curd. Mix the egg yolks with the sugar and the passion fruit seeds in a pan over a medium heat, whisking constantly until warm, then cook for 5 minutes until it creates a thick sauce. Leave to cool.

To finish the mousse, whisk the egg whites with the salt until they form soft peaks and then add the sugar and whisk again until it forms stiff peaks.

Using a spatula, gently fold the egg whites into the curd, keeping in as much air as possible.

Fill 4 glasses with 2 tablespoons of passion fruit curd, then top with the white chocolate mousse.

Keep in the fridge for at least 3 hours, then top with grated coconut or extra passion fruit seeds.

PROFITEROLES FACILES

Easy Homemade Profiteroles

A classic bistro dessert, I think it is a super fun one to make at home when you have guests over! You could serve them all in a serving dish, and leave your guests to top theirs with a saucer filled with the chocolate sauce and a couple of toppings, like roasted flaked almonds, pistachio or hazelnuts.

SERVES 6

For the choux pastry

80g (3oz) butter

150ml (5fl oz/scant ⅔ cup) water

2 tsp caster (superfine) sugar

120g (4oz/1cup) plain (all-purpose) flour

3-4 medium eggs

For the chocolate sauce

150g (5oz) dark patissier chocolate (60/70% cocoa solids)

40g (1½oz) salted butter

150ml (5fl oz/scant ⅔ cup) whole milk

For the filling and decoration

500g (1lb 2oz) your favourite ice cream (I love vanilla, salted caramel, chocolate as a trio)

2 tbsp chopped pistachios

2 tbsp chopped hazelnuts

2 tbsp chopped roasted almonds

To make the choux, melt the butter with the water and sugar in a pan. Add the flour and mix with a wooden spoon, cooking for 2 minutes to dry out the mix, until it forms a ball. Leave to cool for 10 minutes.

Transfer the dough to a food processor, then turn it on, adding 3 eggs, one by one, then check the consistency. If you dip a wooden spoon in, it should create a triangle shape when you lift the spoon up. If it doesn't and is too firm, add an extra egg white to the mix and try again.

Preheat the oven to 200°C fan (220°C/425°F/gas 7).

Fill up a piping bag with the choux pastry, and cut off the tip so you have a 1cm (½in) gap. Pipe 24 x 3-4cm (1¼-1½) choux on a baking sheet and flatten the top of the choux with a fork dipped in water or egg white (so it doesn't stick). Use a pastry brush to brush with egg white.

Bake for 20 minutes, then open the door to let the steam out, then close the door again. Turn off the oven and leave the choux to dry in the cooling oven for 30 minutes to an hour, then remove from the oven and leave to cool completely.

Make the chocolate sauce by melting the chocolate with the butter in a heavy-based pan over a low heat. Then slowly add the milk and use a wooden spoon to mix to a smooth sauce. Set aside.

When it is time to serve your dessert, cut the top off each choux, fill with a scoop of ice cream and replace the top. Pour over the chocolate sauce and sprinkled with nuts to serve.

Tip: You can easily freeze your choux in an airtight container for a few months, so you always have them ready for unexpected guests and you can whip up a quick dessert!

TARTE AUX POMMES DE MAMIE

Mamie's Apple Tart

Baking this tart with my *Mamie* Suzanne is my first true baking memory. I remember making the pastry with her, watching her spread her homemade compote over the pastry and top it with apples peeled and cut by my late grandpa. It is very special to be able to have both my *mamies* sharing their recipes here in this book.

SERVES 4–6

For the pastry

185g (6½oz/scant 1½ cups) plain (all-purpose) flour, plus extra for dusting

1 tsp caster (superfine) sugar

90g (3¼oz) salted butter, diced

2-3 tbsp cold water

4 eating (dessert) apples

2 tsp granulated sugar

For the compôte

4 eating (dessert) apples

25g (¾oz) salted butter

2 tsp sugar

2 tsp water

To make the pastry, mix the flour, sugar and butter together in a bowl. Use your hands to crumble the butter into the flour to make a breadcrumb-like texture. Add the cold water and mix to create a soft pastry. Shape into a ball, cover with clingfilm (plastic wrap) and keep in the fridge until ready to use. To make this quicker, you could also put everything into a food processor and blend for 30 seconds.

For the compôte, simply peel and dice the apples, then cook them with the butter, sugar and water in a pan for 15–20 minutes until softened. Use a fork to mash the compôte, then transfer to a bowl to allow it to cool down.

Remove the pastry from the fridge, lightly flour your benchtop and use a rolling pin to create a large circle of pastry, 2–3mm thick.

Preheat the oven to 180°C fan oven (200°C/400°F/gas 6).

Line your tart tin with the pastry, using your fingers to push it against the tin, and a knife to slice the edge neatly. Prick the surface with a fork.

Peel the 4 apples and slice them thinly.

Spread the compote with a spoon on top of the pastry, arrange the apples on top in the same direction to create a nice pattern. Sprinkle with granulated sugar.

Bake for 45 minutes, or until the crust is golden and the apples are soft and caramelized.

KOUIGN AMANN AUX POMMES

Apple Butter Cake

Meaning literally 'butter cake' in Breton (the Celtic language of Brittany), this is our number one delicacy. Here I have made it with some additional slices of apple in between the layers, creating even more caramelized butteriness.

You will need a 23cm (9in) cake tin.

SERVES 8

275g (9½oz/2¼ cups) strong bread flour, plus extra for dusting

10g (¼oz/2 tsp) melted butter, plus extra for greasing

4g (scant 1 tsp) sea salt

8g (1 sachet) active dried yeast

180ml (6fl oz/¾ cup) water

225g (8oz) salted butter

200g (7oz/heaped 1 cup) caster (superfine) sugar

2 cooking apples, thinly sliced with a mandoline

Combine the flour, melted butter, salt, yeast and the water in a large mixing bowl, and knead the dough for 8 minutes.

Flatten out the butter into a 15cm (6in) square.

Place the dough on a lightly floured work surface and roll it into a 30cm (12in) square using a rolling pin. Place the butter square on top of the dough and close the pastry over the top like a pocket. Roll the dough into a long rectangle. Make the first turn by folding the bottom of the rectangle up to the middle of the rectangle and fold the top of the rectangle to cover that half. Transfer to the fridge to rest for 30 minutes.

Repeat the rolling and folding, but this time scatter the dough rectangle with half of the sugar and half of the thinly sliced apples. Transfer to the fridge to rest for 30 minutes.

Preheat the oven to 180°C fan (200°C/400°F/gas 6). Grease a 23cm (9in) cake tin with butter.

Roll out the dough to a large rectangle once more and generously sprinkle it with the remaining sugar and apples, then roll it up as if you were making cinnamon buns, then cut 6 large rolls. Place the rolls in the buttered tin and cook for 40 minutes until golden.

TO DRINK

The French love their apéritif — the pre-lunch or pre-dinner drink served with some nibbles (like those on pages 198–199) but, depending on the region, there are also other moments in the meal we serve a liquor-based drink. Like a *Trou Normand* (Normandy Apple and Calvados Sorbet, page 237) or a homemade liqueur like *Vin de Pêche* (Peach Wine, page 230), for example. There is also a selection of syrups here (non-alcoholic and alcoholic), which come in handy as you can simply make a Kir with some *Crème de Mûres* (Blackberry Liqueur, page 234) and Champagne or a *Diabolo de Grenadine* (Diabolo with Grenadine, page 231) and lemonade.

VIN DE PÊCHE

Peach Wine

A *Mamie* Gilberte special recipe, she kept this in her little 30-year-old booklet of recipes and notes. It is a great reminder of how smartly we can use nature and what it has to offer. *Mamie* harvests the leaves from her peach tree to make this aperitif wine every year. It tastes almondy and sweet, an easy homemade liquor we love!

**MAKES 5 LITRES
(170FL OZ/20 CUPS)**

100g (3½oz) young fresh peach leaves (harvested in summer)

5 litres (170fl oz/20 cups) red wine (you could also do it with white wine)

1kg (23lb 4oz) caster (superfine) sugar

1 litre (34fl oz/4 cups) eau de vie, Calvados or brandy

Thoroughly wash the leaves with water to remove any dirt.

In a large container with an airtight seal, mix all the ingredients together.

Leave it to macerate for 2 weeks in a cool room, mixing occasionally.

Drain and extract the liquor only.

Keep in dark glass bottles.

Tip: This recipe also works with cherry leaves. You can use the same amount of dried peach and cherry leaves if fresh are not available.

DIABOLO DE GRENADINE

Pomegranate Diabolo

Diabolo is a popular non-alcoholic drink made with lemonade and a fruit syrup. The most classic diabolo flavours you'll find in France will be grenadine, pomegranate and mint. Most French people buy the syrups ready made and simply mix them with some lemonade. Pomegranate syrup is very easy to make and keeps for a long time in the fridge. And here's the perfect soft drink to offer to your summer guests.

SERVES 1

For the grenadine syrup

3 fresh, ripe pomegranates

caster (superfine) sugar the same weight as the pomegranate seeds

For the diabolo

200ml (7fl oz/scant ½ cup) lemonade

Slice the pomegranates in half, then use a heavy spoon to tap the shell and extract the juicy seeds.

Weigh the seeds and put in a bowl with the same weight of sugar and mix roughly together. Cover and keep in the fridge overnight.

Strain the mixture to keep just the juice. Add this juice to a small pan, bring to the boil, then turn the heat down to low and simmer for 10 minutes.

Leave to cool and keep in a glass container in the fridge.

CRÈME DE MÛRES

Blackberry Liqueur

Mamie Suzanne makes this religiously every year. She has a large blackberry bush in her garden with which she makes this and some delicious jams, too. You'll be surprised how easy it is to make and it keeps for at least a year in a sealed glass bottle.

MAKES 2 BOTTLES

1kg (2lb 4oz) blackberries

1 bottle (75cl) red wine

300ml (10fl oz/1¼ cups) vodka or clear alcohol

about 500g (1lb 2oz) granulated sugar

Wash and pour the blackberries into a large bowl with the wine and alcohol, then use your clean hands to mush the blackberries, releasing as much juice as possible. Cover and keep in a cool room, or in the fridge, for 2–3 days to macerate.

After the maceration process, drain all the liquid through a five strainer lined with muslin (cheesecloth), extracting as much juice as possible. Weigh the liquid – which should be around 1kg (2lb 4oz) – then add half the weight of sugar – about 500g (1lb 4oz) – and mix well.

Once the sugar has fully dissolved, fill up your bottles and leave for 2 weeks before serving.

Tip: To make a Kir Royale, add 1 tablespoon of crème de mûres and top it with Champagne or crémant. To make a Kir, it is 1 tablespoon of crème de mûres, topped with white wine.

CRÈME DE CASSIS

Blackcurrant Liqueur

Similar to a *crème de mûres*, the *crème de cassis* is a liqueur you'll find served most often in France. It pairs perfectly with Champagne and gives the cocktail a beautiful colour.

MAKES 2 BOTTLES

1kg (2lb 4oz) blackcurrants

1 bottle (75cl) red wine

300ml (10fl oz1¼ cups) vodka or clear alcohol

about 500g (1lb 2oz) granulated sugar

Wash the blackcurrants, then pour them into a large bowl and add the wine and alcohol, then use your clean hands to mush the blackcurrants, releasing as much juice as possible. Cover and keep in a cool room, or in the fridge, for 5 days, mixing every day.

After the maceration process, drain off all the liquid through a fine strainer lined with muslin (cheesecloth), extracting as much juice as possible. Weigh the liquid – which should be around 1kg (2lb 4oz) – then add half the weight of sugar – about 500g (1lb 4oz) – and mix well.

Place in a large pan, gently bring to boil, then leave to simmer for 5 minutes.

Cool down completely before filling up your bottles. Keep in a cool room.

TROU NORMAND

Normandy Apple and Calvados Sorbet

Trou Normand is a traditional palate cleanser, made simply with apple sorbet topped with Calvados. In my family or around the western regions of France, it is served after the *plat de resistance*, allowing people to have a break before they go on with eating *Les Fromages* and the dessert. It has a special place in my family's heart. My late grandpa used to make his own Calvados, and we still have some 60-year-old bottles to this day. Opening one and enjoying it with the family is always special! The children only eat the sorbet, of course.

SERVES 1

1 scoop of apple sorbet

1 tbsp Calvados

Spoon the sorbet into a small bowl or coupe glass and pour over the Calvados. Serve with a teaspoon.

HOST LIKE
A FRENCH:
MENU PLANS

On TikTok and Instagram, I share my favourite hosting recipes with the hashtag #hostlikeafrench, hence the title of my menu plans! Below is a selection of occasions when you might want to put together a special meal. To make it as stress-free as possible, I have given you some perfect combinations to create superb menus.

Rendez-Vous avec mon Amour
Date Night with my Love

For date nights, I try to focus on quick preparations and minimum stress to make for a lovely evening. You might even want to cook together. Make the dessert in advance and keep it covered in individual glass dishes. Reduce the quantities to make two chicken roulades.

EN ENTRÉE: *Salade Normande* (Normandy Salad, page 83)

EN PLAT: *Médaillons de Poulet d'Automne* (Autumn Stuffed Chicken Breasts, page 134) with *Purée de Pommes de Terre* (Potato Purée, page 181) and a green salad dressed with *Vinaigrette* (Vinaigrette, page 186)

OR

Bavette aux Échalottes (bavette with Shallot Sauce, page 192) with *Frîtes au Four* (Homemade French Fries, page 166)

Get 2 bavette or steaks (150g (5oz) per person) and bring to room temperature. Prepare the *Sauce aux Échallottes* first, and keep it in the pan ready to be reheated. Make the *Frîtes au Four* and keep them warm. When it is time to eat, heat a frying pan with 1 teaspoon of olive oil over a medium–high heat, and fry the bavette for 1–3 minutes (raw, medium rare, well done for each minute) on each side. Season with salt and pepper and serve with the shallot sauce, frîtes and a side of green salad.

EN DESSERT: *Mousse Chocolat Blanc et Fruits de la Passion* (White Chocolate Mousse with Passion Fruit Curd, page 218)

Déjeuner avec les Filles

Lunch with the Girls

I love having my friends over for lunch. I usually focus on making two or three dishes and serve them all together on the table for us to enjoy.

FOR THE VEGETARIAN: *Oeufs Mimosa* (French Devilled Eggs, page 116)

Tartine au Butternut, Fourme d'Ambert et Miel (Butternut, Fourme d'Ambert and Honey Toast, page 73)

Salade de Nectarines, Bufala Mozzarella et Noisettes (Buffalo Mozzarella, Nectarine and Hazelnut Salad, page 45)

FOR THE PESCETARIAN: *Cheesecake au Saumon* (Salmon Cheesecake, page 51)

Salade Croquante de Petit Pois et Haricots (Green Beans and Peas with a Lemon and Basil Dressing, page 158)

FOR THE MEAT EATER: *Quiche Lorraine Facile* (Easy Quiche Lorraine, page 57)

Salade avec Vinaigrette (salad with Vinaigrette, page 186)

Tapenade aux Olives avec Croûtons Aillés (Olive Tapenade with Garlic Crostini, page 92)

Brunch avec la Famille

Family Brunch

For brunch, you can throw anything you enjoy together – there are so many brunch recipes in this book to choose from. The point is to have as many sweet as savoury dishes on your table. This is just a small selection.

Gaufres Sucrées (Sweet Waffles, page 22)

Oeufs Cocotte (Baked Eggs, page 66)

Brioche au Sucre (Sweet Brioche, page 26)

Beurre Salé Breton (Homemade Breton Butter, page 30)

Confiture d'Abricot de Maman (Maman's Apricot Jam, page 39)

Baguette Tradition Facile (Quick Sourdough-like Baguette, page 40)

Un Repas de Fête
A Celebration Meal

We go all out when welcoming friends and family. I know this sounds like an extensive menu ... but it is the reality of what is cooked and served from *Maman*'s kitchen.

EN APERITIF:
Gougères (Cheese Puffs, page 91)

Mini Croissants (Mini Croissants, Tapenade and Sundried Tomato, page 94)

EN ENTRÉE
Soufflé au Fromage (Cheese Souffle, page 104)

EN PLAT:
Saumon en Croûte (page 129) served with *Gratin de Poireaux* (Cheesy Grilled Leeks, page 170) and a sauce Beurre Blanc (White Butter, page 191)

EN FROMAGE:
Serve a *Les Fromages* (Cheeseboard, page 197) with three to five different cheeses and a *salade verte* (green salad)

EN DESSERT:
Îles Flottantes (Floating Islands, page 216)

Pique-nique au Parc
Picnic at the Park

I love a *pique-nique*! In the summer, my parents would often take us for a long bike ride in the forest, before enjoying a pique-nique together down by the lake. We often picked up what was available in the kitchen: fresh baguettes, pâté, cheese and *confiture*.
But on an organised day, *Maman* always made a quiche and a simple salad. They are so easy to transport in big tubs, and simple to serve and enjoy on paper plates.

Mini Croissants Apéro Quatre Façons (Mini Puff Pastry Croissants, Four Ways, page 94)

Quiche aux Légumes (Vegetable Quiche, page 56)

Salade Lyonnaise (Lyon Salad, page 79)

Kouign Amann aux Pommes (Apple Butter Cake, page 226) (often picked up from the boulangerie beforehand) OR *Crêpes* with *Confiture* (Crêpes with Jam, pages 18 and page 39)

A side of bread and some cheese will complete your picnic!

Le Goûter d'Anniversaire

Children's Birthday Party Food

Little people love cute bites and simple flavours. For them, I simply cut the baguette in slices ready to be picked, and I slice and dice the cake too. *Tarte Tropézienne* (page 212) makes such a great birthday cake and is less heavy in sugar than most cakes.

Baguette Surprise (Stuffed Baguette, page 97)

Lasagnes Avec Courgettes et Feta (Vegetarian Courgette and Feta Lasagne, page 130)

Pain au Lait aux Raisins (Raisin Milk Bread, page 33)

Tarte Tropézienne (Tropical Tart, page 212)

INDEX

INDEX

INDEX

MERCI

First of all, I can't believe it is the second time I am writing this section of a book – my book.

I wrote my first book, *Et Voilà!,* whilst organizing my wedding abroad with 180 guests and a one-year-old, and I wrote *Chez Manon* whilst pregnant with my second child (the funny story is that it took as long to create the book as to create my second baby, almost exactly!). So I'd like to say thank you to my husband, Luke, for having supported me throughout, always being my number one fan, pushing me to focus and work harder and better.

Thank you also to the three people who have supported me in my book journey since day one, and continued in the same way for my second book. My manager Joey Swarbrick, my literary agent Antony Topping and my publisher Kate Pollard. Thank you for believing in Manon's Little Kitchen; I hope to create many more books with this dream team.

I was lucky to work again with the most incredible team of creatives for this book. Thanks goes to Nassima Rothacker for your beautiful eye and for capturing the essence of my family and home in Brittany. Frankie Unsworth for your amazing prop finds and food styling visions, and Georgia Rudd for running the smoothest shoot days – you both brought even more French style to the team. Thank you to Jacqui Melville for jumping in and welcoming us in your studio and shooting some stunning recipes for the book. Thank you also to photography assistant Amy Grover, designer Vanessa Masci and to editor Wendy Hobson for dealing with my writing and making it readable. Thanks also to Margaux Durigon for checking my French spelling.

Thank you to Bertrand Larcher for letting the team photograph his galettes and crêpes in his Crêperie La Maison du Sarrasin in Fougères. To Fromagerie Bleu & Crème in Dinard and Jéremie for making us sample his most delicious cheeses. And thanks to Sézane for dressing me throughout the book, French style always.

Finally, thank you to my *maman* and *papa* for welcoming the team into their home last summer, embracing the behind-the-scenes chaos and helping us to make it happen. To *Mamie*, *Papi* and *Mamie* for lending us their field and home, and mostly for being great at modelling for Nassima. To the rest of my Lagrève and Coquelin family for being the best families to grow up with, and the many exquisite meals and moments we continue to share together.